THE CONCISE GUIDE TO
COCKTAILS

THE CONCISE GUIDE TO
COCKTAILS

This is a Parragon Book
First published in 2006

Parragon
Queen Street House
4 Queen Street
Bath BA1 1HE, UK

Designed by Talking Design
Compiled and edited by Julie Whitaker and Ian Whitelaw

ISBN: 1-40547-345-2

Printed in China

measures used in cocktail recipes

Measuring the quantities is one of the keys to a good cocktail. The standard single measure is 25–30 ml, as used in this book, and you can buy stainless steel measures (jiggers) for 1, 2 and ½ quantities in many supermarkets and hardware shops. However, like any good bartender, you can use your own chosen measure as long as you follow the proportions given in the recipes. An appropriately small tumbler, glass or even eggcup will serve as the basic measure. A dash is four or five drops – just enough to add a little colouring or taste.

contents

introduction

The coolest drinks around at the moment are cocktails. They're an invitation to combine fun and creativity with an enduring aura of glamour from the racy 1920s and '30s. You can go into the newest bar in town, most likely to be an imitation of the famous Harry's Bar, to order the latest creation from New York. Or visit the classiest traditional bar around – you can't beat London's Savoy or Manhattan's Algonquin Hotel when it comes to class – and ask for the all-time classic cocktail: a Dry Martini.

The Origin of Cocktails

Precisely where the word 'cocktail' came from is uncertain. A popular piece of folklore describes how a Mexican princess called Xoctl offered a mixed drink to an American visitor to her father's court who confused her name with that of the drink itself. Another suggestion is that the spoon used for mixing drinks reminded imbibing racegoers of the docked tails of non-thoroughbred horses, called cocktails. There are many other flights of fancy, but modern etymologists mostly agree that the word derives from coquetel, a French, wine-based drink.

A Long and Noble History

Whatever the origins of the word cocktail, mixed drinks have existed since ancient times and the first recognizable cocktail dates from about the 16th century. Indeed, many classics have been around for much longer than most people think. The bourbon-based Old Fashioned, for example, first appeared at the end of the 18th century. We know that the word cocktail was already in use in 1809 in the United States and, thirty-five years later, when Charles Dickens described Major Pawkins as able to drink 'more rum-toddy, mint-julep, gin-sling and cock-tail, than any private gentleman of his acquaintance', it had reached Britain, too.

Popular among the style-conscious and wealthy in the United States, cocktails were served before dinner in the most exclusive houses and hotels until World War I made them unfashionable. They have gone in and out of vogue ever since.

The Jazz Era

Following the war, young people, disillusioned by their parents' generation and desperately seeking new experiences, pleasures, stimuli and styles, developed a taste for a new range of cocktails. Ironically, Prohibition in the United States in the 1920s spurred on their development. Illegally produced liquor frequently tasted poisonous – and sometimes was – so its flavour needed to be disguised with fruit juices and mixers. No doubt, the naughtiness of drinking alcoholic cocktails also added to their appeal to the 'bright young things' of the time. The craze quickly crossed the Atlantic, and the best hotels in London, Paris and Monte Carlo, where the quality of gin and whisky was more consistent, soon boasted their own cocktail bars.

Cocktail Revivals

World War II brought an end to such revelry and, although drunk occasionally, cocktails remained out of style for decades until an exuberant renaissance in the 1970s. This resulted in another new generation of recipes, often featuring white rum and vodka, as well as tequila, which was just becoming known outside its native Mexico. Inevitably, the pendulum swung against cocktails again until recently. Now, once more, the cocktail shaker is essential equipment in every fashionable bar.

There's no incomprehensible magic involved in mixing the perfect cocktail. It's a simple matter of combining the prescribed ingredients at the perfect temperature and in the right order, and then serving the delicious result in the correct glass with a little flair. Here's looking at you, kid!

sophisticated classics

tom collins

3 measures gin
2 measures lemon juice
½ measure sugar syrup
4–6 cracked ice cubes
soda water
slice of lemon, to decorate

SERVES 1

This long cooling drink is a celebrated cocktail and was the inspiration for several generations of the Collins drinks family scattered around the globe.

1 Shake the gin, lemon juice and sugar syrup vigorously over ice until well frosted.
2 Strain into a tall chilled tumbler and top up with soda water.
3 Dress with a slice of lemon.

singapore sling

2 measures gin
1 measure cherry brandy
1 measure lemon juice
1 tsp grenadine
4–6 cracked ice cubes
soda water
lime peel and cocktail cherries,
to decorate

SERVES 1

In the days of the British Empire, the privileged
would gather at their clubs in the relative cool
of the evening and sip a Singapore Sling. Times
may change, but it is still the ideal thirst-
quencher on a hot summer's evening.

1 Shake the gin, cherry brandy, lemon juice
and grenadine vigorously over ice until well
frosted.
2 Half fill a chilled highball glass with cracked
ice cubes and strain in the cocktail.
3 Top up with soda water and dress with lime
peel and cocktail cherries.

absinthe friend

1 measure gin
1 measure Pernod
dash Angostura bitters
dash sugar syrup
4–6 cracked ice cubes

SERVES 1

The original absinthe was a popular cocktail ingredient and digestif. However, in the early 20th century absinthe was banned in many countries, as wormwood (one of the main ingredients) was said to react with alcohol and cause brain damage. Any pastis, such as Pernod and Ricard, will do instead.

1 Shake the ingredients vigorously over ice until well frosted.
2 Strain into a chilled medium-size glass or tumbler.

pimm's no.1

ice
1 measure Pimm's No. 1
lemonade
strips of cucumber peel, sprigs of mint or borage, slices of orange and lemon, to decorate

SERVES 1

Pimm's No. 1 is a long, deliciously dry but fruity concoction, with a gin base flavoured with herbs. It was devised by James Pimm, a London restaurateur, in the late 19th century and was quite probably the original Gin Sling.

1 Fill a large chilled glass two-thirds full with ice and pour in the Pimm's.
2 Top up with lemonade and stir gently.
3 Dress with a twist of cucumber peel, a sprig of fresh mint and slices of orange and lemon.

club

4–6 cracked ice cubes
dash of yellow Chartreuse
2 measures gin
1 measure sweet vermouth

SERVES 1

Groucho Marx is well known for claiming that he wouldn't want to belong to any club that was prepared to accept him as a member. This Club and its many associates are unlikely ever to have any shortage of willing members.

1 Put the cracked ice cubes into a mixing glass.
2 Dash the Chartreuse over the ice and pour in the gin and vermouth. Stir well to mix.
3 Strain into a chilled cocktail glass.

dubarry

4–6 cracked ice cubes
dash of Pernod
dash of Angostura bitters
2 measures gin
1 measure dry vermouth
lemon peel twist, to decorate

SERVES 1

The Comtesse du Barry, the mistress of King Louis XV of France, was renowned for her extraordinary beauty. The guillotine brought an abrupt ending to her life – be careful not to lose your head over this delicious concoction.

1 Put the ice cubes into a mixing glass and dash the Pernod and Angostura bitters over them.
2 Pour in the gin and vermouth and stir well to mix.
3 Strain into a chilled cocktail or wine glass and decorate with a twist of lemon.

charleston

¼ measure gin
¼ measure dry vermouth
¼ measure sweet vermouth
¼ measure Cointreau
¼ measure kirsch
¼ measure Maraschino
ice
twist of lemon, to decorate

SERVES 1

This little number combines several tastes and flavours to produce a very lively drink. Don't drink it when you are thirsty, you might want too many!

1 Shake all the ingredients except the lemon together well over ice and strain into a small chilled cocktail glass.
2 Dress with a twist of lemon.

rolls royce

4–6 cracked ice cubes
dash of orange bitters
1 measure dry gin
2 measures dry vermouth
1 measure Scotch whisky

SERVES 1

Hardly surprisingly, several classic cocktails have been named after this classic marque. This version was created by author H. E. Bates in his popular novel *The Darling Buds of May*.

1 Put the cracked ice cubes into a mixing glass.
2 Dash the bitters over the ice.
3 Pour the gin, vermouth and whisky over the ice and stir to mix. Strain into a chilled cocktail glass.

bronx

4–6 cracked ice cubes
2 measures gin
1 measure orange juice
½ measure dry vermouth
½ measure sweet vermouth

SERVES 1

Like Manhattan, the New York borough of the Bronx – and also the river of the same name – have been immortalised in cocktail bars throughout the world.

1 Put the cracked ice cubes into a mixing glass.
2 Pour the gin, orange juice and dry and sweet vermouth over the ice. Stir to mix.
3 Strain into a chilled cocktail glass.

alexander

4–6 cracked ice cubes
1 measure gin
1 measure crème de cacao
1 measure single cream
freshly grated nutmeg,
to decorate

SERVES 1

This creamy, chocolate-flavoured, gin-based cocktail, decorated with grated nutmeg, is the head of an extended family of cocktails, which continues to grow.

1 Put the cracked ice cubes into a cocktail shaker.
2 Pour the gin, crème de cacao and single cream over the ice. Shake vigorously until a frost forms.
3 Strain into a chilled cocktail glass and sprinkle with the nutmeg.

orange blossom

4–6 cracked ice cubes
2 measures gin
2 measures orange juice
slice of orange, to decorate

SERVES 1

It is disappointing to discover that the pretty name of this cocktail is derived from the practice of adding fresh orange juice to bathtub gin during the years of Prohibition in the United States in order to conceal its filthy flavour. Made with good-quality gin, which needs no such concealment, it is delightfully refreshing.

1 Put the cracked ice cubes into a cocktail shaker.
2 Pour the gin and orange juice over the ice and shake vigorously until a frost forms.
3 Strain into a chilled cocktail glass and decorate with the orange slice.

white lady

2 measures gin
1 measure Triple Sec
1 measure lemon juice
4–6 cracked ice cubes

SERVES 1

Simple, elegant, subtle and much more powerful than appearance suggests, this is the perfect cocktail to serve before an al fresco summer dinner.

1 Shake the gin, Triple Sec and lemon juice vigorously over ice until well frosted.
2 Strain into a chilled cocktail glass.

rickey

4–6 cracked ice cubes
2 measures gin
1 measure lime juice
soda water, to top up
slice of lemon, to decorate

SERVES 1

The classic version of this cocktail is based on gin, but other spirits are also used, mixed with lime or lemon juice and soda water with no sweetening.

1 Put the cracked ice cubes into a chilled highball glass or goblet.
2 Pour the gin and lime juice over the ice. Top up with soda water.
3 Stir gently to mix and decorate with the lemon slice.

maiden's blush

4–6 cracked ice cubes
2 measures gin
½ tsp Triple Sec
½ tsp grenadine
½ tsp lemon juice

SERVES 1

The name of this cocktail aptly describes its pretty colour. Drink too many, however, and maidenly modesty may be abandoned and blushing could become compulsory.

1 Put the cracked ice cubes into a cocktail shaker.
2 Pour the gin, Triple Sec, grenadine and lemon juice over the ice. Shake vigorously until a frost forms.
3 Strain into a chilled cocktail glass or small highball glass.

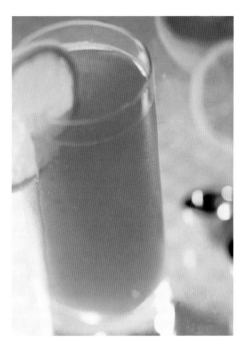

daisy

3 measures gin
1 measure lemon juice
1 tbsp grenadine
1 tsp sugar syrup
4–6 cracked ice cubes
soda water
slice of orange, to decorate

SERVES 1

A Daisy is a long cocktail with a high proportion of alcohol and sweetened with fruit syrup. Perhaps it gets its name from the now old-fashioned slang when the word 'daisy' referred to something exceptional and special.

1 Pour the gin, lemon juice, grenadine and sugar syrup over the cracked ice and shake vigorously until well frosted.
2 Strain into a chilled highball glass and top up with soda water.
3 Stir gently, then decorate with an orange slice.

gin sling

1 cube sugar
1 measure dry gin
freshly grated nutmeg
slice of lemon, to decorate

SERVES 1

Many say the original gin sling was hot, but there are numerous cool variations to enjoy too!

1 Dissolve the sugar in 150ml/5 fl oz hot water in an old-fashioned glass.
2 Stir in the gin, sprinkle with nutmeg and serve with a slice of lemon.

martini

3 measures gin
1 tsp dry vermouth,
or to taste
4–6 cracked ice cubes
olive, to decorate

SERVES 1

For many, this is the ultimate cocktail. It is named after its inventor, Martini de Anna de Toggia, not the famous brand of vermouth!

1 Pour the gin and vermouth over cracked ice in a mixing glass and stir well to mix.
2 Strain into a chilled cocktail glass and dress with a cocktail olive.

dry martini

1 measure London
Dry gin
dash dry vermouth
a single olive or a
twist of lemon, to
decorate

SERVES 1

Unlike the Martini, this drink has almost no vermouth in. Traditionalists will tell you simply to wave the bottle over the glass!

1 Stir the gin and vermouth over a handful of ice in a stirring glass.
2 Stir well and strain into a cocktail glass.
3 Dress simply with a single olive or a twist of lemon.

pink gin

1 measure Plymouth gin
few drops Angostura bitters
1 measure iced water
maraschino cherry,
to decorate

SERVES 1

Originally devised as a remedy for stomach complaints, the Pink Gin was subsequently adopted by the British Navy as part of its medicine chest.

1 Pour the first three ingredients into a mixing glass and stir.
2 Strain into a cocktail glass and garnish with a maraschino cherry.

negroni

This aristocratic cocktail was created by Count Negroni at the Bar Giacosa in Florence, although since then, the proportions of gin to Campari have altered.

4–6 cracked ice cubes
1 measure Campari
1 measure gin
½ measure sweet vermouth
twist of orange peel, to decorate

SERVES 1

1 Put the cracked ice cubes into a mixing glass.
2 Pour the Campari, gin and vermouth over the ice. Stir well to mix.
3 Strain into a chilled glass and decorate with the orange twist.

cosmopolitan

2 measures vodka
1 measure Triple Sec
1 measure fresh lime juice
1 measure cranberry juice
orange peel, to decorate

SERVES 1

This contemporary classic, made famous by the TV show *Sex in the City*, is the only drink to serve at a trendy party!

1 Shake all the ingredients over ice until well frosted.
2 Strain into a chilled cocktail glass.
3 Dress with a strip of orange peel.

screwdriver

4–6 cracked ice cubes
2 measures vodka
orange juice, to top up
slice of orange, to decorate

SERVES 1

Always use freshly squeezed orange juice to make this refreshing cocktail – it is just not the same with bottled juice. This simple, classic cocktail has given rise to numerous and increasingly elaborate variations.

1 Fill a chilled glass with cracked ice cubes.
2 Pour the vodka over the ice and top up with orange juice.
3 Stir well to mix and dress with a slice of orange.

fuzzy navel

2 measures vodka
1 measure peach schnapps
250ml/8 fl oz orange juice
4–6 cracked ice cubes
physalis (cape gooseberry),
to decorate

SERVES 1

This is one of those cocktails with a name that plays on the ingredients – fuzzy to remind you that it contains peach schnapps and navel because it is mixed with orange juice.

1 Shake the vodka, peach schnapps and orange juice vigorously over cracked ice until well frosted.
2 Strain into a chilled cocktail glass and dress with a physalis.

salty dog

1 tbsp granulated sugar
1 tbsp coarse salt
lime wedge
6–8 cracked ice cubes
2 measures vodka
grapefruit juice, to top up

SERVES 1

This is another cocktail that has changed since its invention. When it first appeared, gin-based cocktails were by far the most popular, but nowadays, a Salty Dog is more frequently made with vodka. You can use either spirit, but the cocktails will have different flavours.

1 Mix the sugar and salt in a saucer.
2 Rub the rim of a chilled Collins glass with the lime wedge, then dip it in the sugar and salt mixture to frost.
3 Fill the glass with cracked ice cubes and pour the vodka over them.
4 Top up with grapefruit juice and stir to mix. Serve with a straw.

kamikaze

1 measure vodka
1 measure Triple Sec
½ measure fresh lime juice
½ measure fresh lemon juice
ice
dry white wine, chilled,
to top up
piece of lime and cucumber,
to decorate

SERVES 1

No turning back on this one. It's so delicious –
you won't be able to put it down.

1 Shake the first four ingredients together over
ice until well frosted.
2 Strain into a chilled glass and top up
with wine.
3 Dress with lime and cucumber.

moscow mule

2 measures vodka
1 measure lime juice
4–6 cracked ice cubes
ginger beer, to top up
slice of lime, to decorate

SERVES 1

This cocktail came about by sheer chance during
the 1930s. An American bar owner had
overstocked on ginger beer, and a representative
of the soft drinks company invented the Moscow
Mule to help him out.

1 Shake the vodka and lime juice vigorously over
ice until well frosted.
2 Half fill a chilled highball glass with cracked ice
cubes and strain the cocktail over them.
3 Top up with ginger beer. Dress with a slice of
lime.

black russian

2 measures vodka
1 measure coffee liqueur
4–6 cracked ice cubes

SERVES 1

History records only White and Red Russians. The omission of the Black Russian is a sad oversight. For a coffee liqueur, you can use either Tia Maria or Kahlúa, depending on your personal taste – the latter is sweeter.

1 Pour the vodka and liqueur over cracked ice cubes in a small chilled highball glass.
2 Stir to mix.

harvey wallbanger

ice cubes
3 measures vodka
8 measures orange juice
2 tsp Galliano
cherry and slice of orange, to
decorate

SERVES 1

This well-known classic cocktail is a great party drink – mix it strong at first, then weaker as the evening goes by – or without alcohol for drivers and no one would know...!

1 Half fill a highball glass with ice, pour vodka and orange over the ice cubes, and float Galliano on top.
2 Garnish with a cherry and slice of orange.

bloody mary

dash Worcestershire sauce
dash Tabasco sauce
4–6 cracked ice cubes
2 measures vodka
splash dry sherry
6 measures tomato juice
juice of half a lemon
pinch celery salt
pinch cayenne pepper
celery stick with leaves,
slice of lemon, to decorate

SERVES 1

This classic cocktail was invented in 1921 at the legendary Harry's Bar in Paris. There are numerous versions – some much hotter and spicier. Ingredients may include horseradish sauce in addition to, or instead of, Tabasco sauce.

1 Dash the Worcestershire sauce and Tabasco sauce over ice in a cocktail shaker and add the vodka, splash of dry sherry, tomato juice and lemon juice.
2 Shake vigorously until frosted.
3 Strain into a tall chilled glass, add a pinch of celery salt and a pinch of cayenne and decorate with a celery stick and a slice of lemon.

long island iced tea

2 measures vodka
1 measure gin
1 measure white tequila
1 measure white rum
½ measure white
crème de menthe
2 measures lemon juice
1 tsp sugar syrup
cracked ice cubes
cola, to top up
wedge of lime or lemon,
to decorate

SERVES 1

Dating back to the days of the American Prohibition, when it was drunk out of cups in an attempt to fool the FBI that it was harmless, this cocktail has evolved from the original simple combination of vodka with a dash of cola!

1 Shake the vodka, gin, tequila, rum, crème de menthe, lemon juice and sugar syrup vigorously over ice until well frosted.
2 Strain into an ice-filled highball glass and top up with cola.
3 Dress with a lime or lemon wedge.

rusty nail

4–6 cracked ice cubes
1 measure Scotch whisky
1 measure Drambuie

SERVES 1

One of the great classic cocktails, so simple and very popular. It must be served on the rocks.

1 Fill an old-fashioned glass or low tumbler half full with ice.
2 Pour in the whisky and Drambuie and stir well.

old fashioned

sugar cube
dash of Angostura bitters
1 tsp water
2 measures bourbon or rye
whiskey
4–6 cracked ice cubes
lemon peel twist, to decorate

SERVES 1

So ubiquitous is this cocktail that a small, straight-sided tumbler is known as an old-fashioned glass. It is a perfect illustration of the saying, 'Sometimes the old ones are the best.'

1 Place the sugar cube in a small, chilled old-fashioned glass. Dash the bitters over the cube and add the water. Mash with a spoon until the sugar has dissolved.
2 Pour the bourbon or rye whiskey into the glass and stir. Add the cracked ice cubes and decorate with the lemon twist.

whisky mac

1½ measures Scotch whisky
1 measure ginger wine

SERVES 1

This popular classic is enjoyed worldwide as a warming winter drink, so don't be tempted to chill the glass or the drinks.

1 Carefully pour ingredients into an old-fashioned glass and allow to mix but don't stir.

blood and sand

1 measure whiskey
1 measure cherry brandy
1 measure red vermouth
ice
orange juice, to top up

SERVES 1

Originating in the American South and using some of the best American whiskey, this classic can also be made with vodka, gin or other spirits.

1 Shake the first three ingredients over ice until frosted.
2 Strain into a medium-size glass and top up with orange juice.

manhattan

4–6 cracked ice cubes
dash Angostura bitters
3 measures rye whiskey
1 measure sweet vermouth
cocktail cherry, to decorate

SERVES 1

Said to have been invented by Sir Winston Churchill's American mother, Jennie, the Manhattan is one of many cocktails named after places in New York.

1 Stir the liquids over cracked ice in a mixing glass and mix well.
2 Strain into a chilled glass and decorate with the cherry.

whiskey sour

4–6 cracked ice cubes
2 measures American blended whiskey
1 measure lemon juice
1 tsp sugar syrup
cocktail cherry,
slice of orange, to decorate

SERVES 1

Sours are short drinks, flavoured with lemon or lime juice. They can be made with almost any spirit, although Whiskey Sour was the original and, for many, is still the favourite.

1 Put the cracked ice into a cocktail shaker.
2 Pour the whiskey, lemon juice and sugar syrup over the ice. Shake vigorously until a frost forms.
3 Strain into a chilled cocktail glass and decorate with the cherry and orange slice.

mint julep

fresh mint leaves
1 tbsp sugar syrup
6–8 crushed ice cubes
3 measures bourbon whiskey
fresh mint sprig, to decorate

SERVES 1

A julep is simply a mixed drink sweetened with syrup – but the mere word conjures up images of ante-bellum cotton plantations and a long-gone, leisurely and gracious way of life.

1 Put the mint leaves and sugar syrup into a small, chilled glass and mash with a teaspoon. Add crushed ice to fill the tumbler, then add the bourbon.
2 Decorate with the mint sprig.

zombie

4–6 crushed ice cubes
2 measures dark rum
2 measures white rum
1 measure golden rum
1 measure Triple Sec
1 measure lime juice
1 measure orange juice
1 measure pineapple juice
1 measure guava juice
1 tbsp grenadine
1 tbsp orgeat
1 tsp Pernod
sprigs of fresh mint and
pineapple wedges, to decorate

SERVES 1

The individual ingredients of this cocktail, including liqueurs and fruit juices, vary considerably from one recipe to another, but all Zombies contain a mixture of white, golden and dark rum in varying proportions.

1 Put crushed ice in a blender with all but the mint and pineapple.
2 Blend until smooth.
3 Pour, without straining, into a chilled Collins glass and dress with mint and a wedge of pineapple.

acapulco

10–12 cracked ice cubes
2 measures white rum
½ measure Triple Sec
½ measure lime juice
1 tsp sugar syrup
1 egg white
sprig of fresh mint, to decorate

SERVES 1

This is one of many cocktails that has changed from its original recipe over the years. To begin with, it was always rum-based and did not include any fruit juice. Nowadays, it is increasingly made with tequila, because this has become better known outside its native Mexico.

1 Put 4–6 cracked ice cubes into a cocktail shaker.
2 Pour the rum, Triple Sec, lime juice and sugar syrup over the ice and add the egg white. Shake vigorously until a frost forms.
3 Half fill a chilled highball glass with cracked ice cubes and strain the cocktail over them. Decorate with the mint sprig.

mai tai

4–6 cracked ice cubes
2 measures white rum
2 measures dark rum
1 measure clear Curaçao
1 measure lime juice
1 tbsp orgeat
1 tbsp grenadine
slices of pineapple,
cocktail cherries,
orchid, to decorate

SERVES 1

This cocktail always inspires elaborate decoration – sometimes so much so that you can be in danger of stabbing your nose on a cocktail stick when you try to drink it. If you want to go completely over the top with decorations – and why not – serving the drink with one or two long, colourful straws might be a good idea.

1 Put the cracked ice cubes into a cocktail shaker.
2 Pour the white and dark rums, Curaçao, lime juice, orgeat and grenadine over the ice. Shake vigorously until a frost forms.
3 Strain into a chilled Collins glass and decorate with the pineapple and cherries, adding an orchid if desired.

daiquiri

2 measures white rum
¾ measure lime juice
½ tsp sugar syrup
cracked ice

SERVES 1

Daiquiri is a town in Cuba, where this drink was said to have been invented in the early part of the 20th century. A businessman had run out of imported gin and so had to make do with the local drink – rum – which, at that time, was often of unreliable quality.

1 Pour the rum, lime juice and sugar syrup over ice and shake vigorously until well frosted.
2 Strain into a chilled cocktail glass.

planter's punch

10–12 cracked ice cubes
dash of grenadine
2 measures white rum
2 measures dark rum
1 measure lemon juice
1 measure lime juice
1 tsp sugar syrup
¼ tsp Triple Sec
sparkling mineral water,
to top up
slices of lemon, lime,
and pineapple and
cocktail cherry, to decorate

SERVES 1

Derived from a Hindi word meaning five, punch is so called because, traditionally, it contained five ingredients. These should also include four basic flavours – strong, weak, sour and sweet.

1 Put 4–6 cracked ice cubes into a cocktail shaker. Dash the grenadine over the ice and pour in the white rum, dark rum, lemon juice, lime juice, sugar syrup and Triple Sec. Shake vigorously until a frost forms.
2 Half fill a tall, chilled Collins glass with cracked ice cubes and strain the cocktail over them. Top up with sparkling mineral water and stir gently.
3 Decorate with the lemon, lime and pineapple slices and a cherry.

cuba libre

4–6 cracked ice cubes
2 measures white rum
cola, to top up
wedge of lime, to decorate

SERVES 1

The 1960s and 1970s saw the meteoric rise in popularity of this simple, long drink, perhaps because of highly successful marketing by Bacardi brand rum, the original white Cuban rum (now produced in the Bahamas) and Coca-Cola, but more likely because rum and cola seem to be natural companions.

1 Half fill a highball glass with cracked ice cubes.
2 Pour the rum over the ice and top up with cola.
3 Stir gently to mix and decorate with a lime wedge.

pinacolada

4–6 crushed ice cubes
2 measures white rum
1 measure dark rum
3 measures pineapple juice
2 measures coconut cream
pineapple wedges,
to decorate

SERVES 1

One of the younger generation of classics, this became popular during the cocktail revival of the 1980s and has remained so ever since.

1 Whizz the crushed ice in a blender with the white rum, dark rum, pineapple juice and coconut cream until smooth.
2 Pour, without straining, into a tall chilled glass and dress with pineapple wedges.

stinger

4–6 cracked ice cubes
2 measures brandy
1 measure white crème de
menthe

SERVES 1

Aptly named, this is a refreshing, clean-tasting cocktail to tantalise the taste buds and make you sit up and take notice. However, bear in mind that it packs a punch and if you have too many, you are likely to keel over.

1 Put the ice cubes into a cocktail shaker. Pour the brandy and crème de menthe over the ice. Shake vigorously until a frost forms.
2 Strain into a small, chilled highball glass.

sidecar

2 measures brandy
1 measure orange-
flavoured liqueur
1 measure lemon juice
4–6 cracked ice cubes
orange slice,
to decorate

SERVES 1

Cointreau is the best-known brand of the orange-flavoured liqueur, or you could use Triple Sec. It is drier and stronger than Curaçao and is always colourless.

1 Put the ice into a cocktail shaker.
2 Pour the brandy, Triple Sec and lemon juice over ice and shake vigorously until a frost forms.
3 Strain into a chilled glass and dress with a slice of orange.

b and b

4–6 cracked ice cubes
1 measure brandy
1 measure Bénédictine

SERVES 1

Although elaborate concoctions are great fun to mix – and drink – some of the best cocktails are the simplest. B & B – brandy and Bénédictine – couldn't be easier, but it has a superbly subtle flavour.

1 Put the ice cubes into a mixing glass. Pour the brandy and Bénédictine over the ice and stir to mix.
2 Strain into a chilled cocktail glass.

between the sheets

8–10 cracked ice cubes
4 measures brandy
3 measures white rum
1 measure clear Curaçao
1 measure lemon juice

SERVES 2

As the name of this cocktail always seems to imply romance and hints that the sheets in question are, at the very least, satin, make it for two people. Certainly, this delicious concoction is as smooth as silk.

1 Put the cracked ice into a cocktail shaker. Pour the brandy, rum, Curaçao and lemon juice over the ice. Shake vigorously until a frost forms.
2 Strain into two chilled wine glasses or goblets.

american rose

4–6 cracked ice cubes
1½ measures brandy
1 tsp grenadine
½ tsp Pernod
½ fresh peach, peeled and mashed
sparkling wine, to top up
fresh peach wedge, to decorate

SERVES 1

'A rose by any other name...' – this pretty cocktail has, rightly, inspired roses across the world. It is truly a thing of beauty and a joy forever.

1 Put the cracked ice in a cocktail shaker. Pour the brandy, grenadine and Pernod over the ice and add the peach. Shake vigorously until a frost forms.
2 Strain into a chilled wine goblet and top up with sparkling wine. Stir gently, then garnish with the peach wedge.

classic cocktail

wedge of lemon
1 tsp caster sugar
4–6 cracked ice cubes
2 measures brandy
½ measure clear Curaçao
½ measure Maraschino
½ measure lemon juice
lemon slice, to decorate

SERVES 1

It cannot lay claim to being the first or even the only classic, but it has all the characteristic hallmarks of sophistication associated with cocktails.

1 Rub the rim of a chilled cocktail glass with the lemon wedge and then dip in the sugar to frost.

2 Put the cracked ice into a cocktail shaker. Pour the brandy, Curaçao, Maraschino and lemon juice over the ice and shake vigorously until a frost forms.

3 Strain into the frosted glass and decorate with the lemon slice.

brandy alexander

1 measure brandy
1 measure dark crème
de cacao
1 measure double cream
ice
grated nutmeg, to decorate

SERVES 1

A lovely creamy concoction that is popular as an after-dinner cocktail. The original was the Alexander, a gin-based drink.

1 Shake the brandy, crème de cacao and cream vigorously over ice until well frosted.
2 Strain into a chilled cocktail glass and dress with a sprinkling of grated nutmeg.

egg nog

1 egg
1 tbsp caster sugar
2 measures brandy or your favourite spirit
milk, warm or cooling
grated nutmeg, to decorate

SERVES 1

The perfect lift when recovering, and a marvellous energy boost when you're feeling a little bit under the weather.

1 Whisk the first three ingredients together, strain into a tall glass and top up with milk.
2 Sprinkle with freshly grated nutmeg.

brave bull

4–6 cracked ice cubes
2 measures white tequila
1 measure Tia Maria
spiral of lemon peel,
to decorate

SERVES 1

Spain's historical associations with Mexico has left many legacies – not least a taste for bullfighting – although whether this cocktail is named in tribute to the animal or because it makes the drinker proverbially brave is anyone's guess.

1 Put the cracked ice into a mixing glass. Pour the tequila and Tia Maria over the ice and stir well to mix.
2 Strain into a chilled goblet and decorate with the spiral of lemon peel.

tequila sunrise

2 measures silver tequila
4–6 cracked ice cubes
orange juice, to top up
1 measure grenadine

SERVES 1

This is one cocktail you shouldn't rush when making, or you will spoil the attractive sunrise effect produced by the grenadine slowly spreading through the orange juice.

1 Pour the tequila over cracked ice in a chilled highball glass and top up with the orange juice. Stir well to mix.
2 Slowly pour in the grenadine and serve with a straw.

margarita

lime wedge
coarse salt
4–6 cracked ice cubes
3 measures white tequila
1 measure Triple Sec
2 measures lime juice
slice of lime, to decorate

SERVES 1

The traditional way to drink tequila is to shake a little salt on the back of your hand between the thumb and forefinger and, holding a wedge of lime or lemon, lick the salt, suck the fruit and then down a shot of tequila in one. This cocktail, attributed to Francisco Morales and invented in 1942 in Mexico, is a more civilised version.

1 Rub the rim of a chilled cocktail glass with the lime wedge and then dip in a saucer of coarse salt to frost.
2 Put the cracked ice cubes into a cocktail shaker. Pour the tequila, Triple Sec and lime juice over the ice. Shake vigorously until a frost forms.
3 Strain into the prepared glass and decorate with the lime slice.

sherry cobbler

6–8 cracked ice cubes
¼ tsp sugar syrup
¼ tsp clear Curaçao
4 measures Amontillado
sherry
pineapple wedges,
twist of lemon peel, to
decorate

SERVES 1

A long drink made with syrup and fresh fruit garnishes, Sherry Cobbler is the original, but there are now numerous and often more potent variations.

1 Fill a wine glass with crushed ice. Add the sugar syrup and Curaçao and stir until a frost forms.
2 Pour in the sherry and stir well. Decorate with pineapple wedges speared on a cocktail stick and the lemon twist.

contemporary favourites

road runner

4–6 cracked ice cubes
2 measures gin
½ measure dry vermouth
½ measure Pernod
1 tsp grenadine

SERVES 1

Whether it is named after the real bird or after Bugs Bunny's famous companion, this is a cocktail for slowing down after a fast-moving day, not for speeding things up.

1 Put the cracked ice into a cocktail shaker.
2 Pour the gin, vermouth, Pernod and grenadine over the ice. Shake vigorously until a frost forms.
3 Strain into a chilled wine glass.

bleu bleu bleu

1 measure gin
1 measure vodka
1 measure tequila
1 measure blue Curaçao
1 measure fresh lemon juice
2 dashes egg white
crushed ice
soda water

SERVES 1

It may well be blurr blurr after this heady combination, so don't rush for the second one.

1 Shake all ingredients except the soda water together over ice until frosted.
2 Pour into a tall glass filled with ice and top up with soda water to taste.

mah-jong

1 measure gin
¼ measure Cointreau
¼ measure white rum
ice
strip of orange peel,
to decorate

SERVES 1

No Chinese games here, and you may not be walking in perfect straight lines if you drink too many!

1 Stir all the ingredients over ice in a mixing glass and strain into a chilled small cocktail glass.
2 Dress with a piece of orange peel.

golden dawn

½ measure gin
½ measure Calvados
½ measure apricot brandy
½ measure mango juice
ice
dash grenadine

SERVES 1

Like the sun rising over a tropical beach, the glow of the grenadine peeps through the brandy and orange.

1 Mix the first four ingredients together over ice.
2 Strain into a cocktail glass and gradually add a dash of grenadine so the colour ripples through.

bird of paradise

1 thick slice watermelon – save a piece to decorate
1 measure gin, chilled
1 measure passion fruit nectar, chilled
½ measure orange Curaçao, chilled
crushed ice

SERVES 1

This is sometimes made with blue Curaçao, but orange Curaçao gives a much more appetising finishing colour. However, it's up to you, so try them both!

1 Deseed the watermelon.
2 Blend all the ingredients together with the ice until partly frozen.
3 Pour into a tumbler or large cocktail glass and dress with a wedge of melon. You may need a spoon!

mississippi fizz

2 measures gin
1 measure fresh lime juice
1 measure passion fruit juice
¼ measure syrop de gomme
3 dashes orange flower water
1 measure soda water
crushed ice

SERVES 1

This fizz is packed with fruity flavours and a subtle taste of frozen gin.

1 Whizz all the ingredients together in a blender on fast for a few seconds or until really frothy.
2 Pour into a large iced cocktail glass or highball glass and serve with a straw.

fallen angel

1 dash Angostura bitters
juice of 1 lemon or lime
2 measures gin
ice
2 dashes green
crème de menthe

SERVES 1

Mint and lemon make an unusual addition to gin, but do make sure it is a green mint liqueur or it will not have the same visual impact.

1 Shake the first three ingredients well over ice and strain into a cocktail glass.
2 Top with two dashes of crème de menthe at the last minute.

bulldog

2 measure gin
1 measure fresh orange juice
ice
ginger ale
slice of orange

SERVES 1

A refreshing variation on the classic gin and orange.

1 Stir the gin and orange over ice in a medium tumbler.
2 Top up with ginger ale and add a slice of orange.

cat's eye

4–6 cracked ice cubes
2 measures gin
1½ measures dry vermouth
½ measure kirsch
½ measure Triple Sec
½ measure lemon juice
½ measure water

SERVES 1

A cat's eye is many things – apart from what a cat sees with – including a semi-precious stone and a stripy marble. Now, it's a highly potent cocktail, as pretty as a gemstone and certainly more fun than playing marbles.

1 Put the cracked ice cubes into a cocktail shaker. Pour the gin, vermouth, kirsch, Triple Sec, lemon juice and water over the ice.
2 Shake vigorously until a frost forms. Strain into a chilled goblet.

vodkatini

1 measure vodka
ice
dash dry vermouth
a single olive or a twist of lemon

SERVES 1

The celebrated 007 popularised the use of vodka as the base of the Martini, rather than gin, hence the Vodkatini is now widely accepted as an incredibly stylish and tasty alternative.

1 Pour the vodka over a handful of ice in a mixing glass.
2 Add the vermouth, stir well and strain into a cocktail glass.
3 Dress with a single olive or a twist of lemon.

chilly willy

2 measures vodka
1 tsp chopped fresh chilli
cracked ice cubes

SERVES 1

Truly a cocktail for the brave-hearted – the heat depends on the type of chilli (some are much more fiery than others) as well as the quantity you add and whether the chilli was deseeded first. For an even spicier cocktail, use chilli vodka as well!

1 Shake the vodka over ice with the chilli until a frost forms.
2 Strain into a small chilled tumbler.

golden tang

2 measures vodka
1 measure Strega
½ measure crème de banane
½ measure orange squash
cracked ice
cherry and orange slice

SERVES 1

Summery colours combine with the autumnal flavours of fruit and herbs to produce a delicious and refreshing mix.

1 Shake the first four ingredients together over ice until well frosted.
2 Strain into chilled glass and dress with a cherry and slice of orange.

bay breeze

2 measures white cranberry
and apple juice
2 measures pineapple juice
2 measures vodka
ice
tonic water
slices of lime or pineapple, to
decorate

SERVES 1

The new white cranberry juices are perfect for
mixing a refreshing cocktail combination. Not
as sharp as red cranberry, but deliciously fruity.

1 Shake the first three ingredients well over ice
until frosted.
2 Strain into a tall glass and top up with tonic
to taste.
3 Dress with slices of lime or pineapple.

sea breeze

1½ measures vodka
½ measure cranberry juice
ice
pink grapefruit juice, to taste

SERVES 1

Pink grapefruit juice is much sweeter and
subtler than its paler cousin, so it is ideal to mix
in cocktails where you want just a slight
sharpness.

1 Shake the vodka and cranberry juice over ice
until frosted.
2 Pour into a chilled tumbler or long glass and
top up with grapefruit juice to taste.
3 Serve with a straw.

angelic

1 measure vodka
½ measure Galliano
½ measure Southern Comfort
dash egg white
ice
orange or pineapple
juice, to taste
slice of pineapple, to decorate

SERVES 1

It may look angelic, but, unless you are very liberal with the fruit juice, this is certainly not a mild cocktail.

1 Shake the first four ingredients over ice until well frosted.
2 Strain into an ice-filled tall glass and top up with orange or pineapple juice to taste.
3 Dress with a slice of fresh pineapple.

dry smile

1 measure mandarin vodka
1 measure Cinzano extra dry
½ measure orange Curaçao
juice ½ lemon
1 tbsp strawberry syrup
ice
pineapple juice, to taste
strawberry, to decorate

SERVES 1

If you like really dry mixes, go easy on the pineapple juice until you have tasted it.

1 Shake the first five ingredients well over ice.
2 Pour into a long glass and top up with pineapple juice to taste.
3 Finish with a slice of strawberry.

full monty

1 measure vodka
1 measure Galliano
4–6 cracked ice cubes
grated ginseng root (use root
ginger if you can't find ginseng),
to decorate

SERVES 1

The expression 'full monty' – meaning not
holding anything back – has been around for a
long time, but was given a new lease of life by
the highly successful British film of the same title.
However, you can keep your clothes on when
drinking this.

1 Shake the vodka and Galliano vigorously over
ice until well frosted.
2 Strain into a chilled cocktail glass and sprinkle
with grated ginseng root.

cinnamon park

1 measure vodka
2 measures pink grapefruit
juice
⅛ measure Campari
1 dash syrop de gomme
pinch or two cinnamon
1 egg white
ice

SERVES 1

Cinnamon and other spices can make all the
difference to fruit-based cocktails. Add to taste or
sprinkle on the top before drinking.

1 Shake all the ingredients well over ice and
strain into a chilled medium-sized cocktail glass.

vodga

4–6 cracked ice cubes
2 measures vodka
1 measure Strega
½ measure orange juice

SERVES 1

As a rule, classic cocktails based on vodka were intended to provide the kick of an alcoholic drink with no tell-tale signs on the breath and they were usually fairly simple mixes of fruit juice, sodas and other non-alcoholic flavourings. By contrast, contemporary cocktails based on vodka often include other aromatic and flavoursome spirits and liqueurs, with vodka adding extra strength.

1 Put the cracked ice cubes into a cocktail shaker.
2 Pour the vodka, Strega and orange juice over the ice. Shake vigorously until a frost forms.
3 Strain into a chilled cocktail glass.

russian double

1 measure red vodka, iced
strips of lemon or orange peel
1 measure lemon vodka or
schnapps, iced

SERVES 1

Vodka and schnapps are both very strong
drinks, so handle with care!

1 Layer the drinks carefully in a chilled shot
glass, putting a piece of peel in the first layer,
and drink immediately.

polynesian pepper pot

4–6 cracked ice cubes
dash of Tabasco sauce
2 measures vodka
1 measure golden rum
4 measures pineapple juice
½ measure orgeat
1 tsp lemon juice
¼ tsp cayenne pepper
pinch of curry powder, to decorate

SERVES 1

It may seem strange to make a sweet drink and then season it with pepper and spices, but there is a long and honourable culinary tradition of making the most of the slightly acerbic flavour of pineapple in this kind of way.

1 Put the cracked ice into a cocktail shaker. Dash Tabasco sauce over the ice, pour in the vodka, rum, pineapple juice, orgeat and lemon juice and add the cayenne. Shake vigorously until a frost forms.
2 Strain into a chilled glass and sprinkle curry powder on top.

seeing red

1 measure red vodka
1 measure peach schnapps
3 measures cranberry juice
crushed ice
soda water
frozen cranberries

SERVES 1

There is a real kick to this cocktail, and the cranberry juice imparts a wonderfully vivid colour.

1 Shake the first three ingredients over ice until well frosted.
2 Strain into a tall chilled cocktail glass, top up with soda water and float a few frozen cranberries on the top.

crocodile

4–6 cracked ice cubes
2 measures vodka
1 measure Triple Sec
1 measure Midori
2 measures lemon juice

SERVES 1

This is certainly a snappy cocktail with a bit of bite. However, it probably gets its name from its spectacular colour – Midori, a Japanese melon-flavoured liqueur, which is a startling shade of green.

1 Put the cracked ice cubes into a cocktail shaker.
2 Pour the vodka, Triple Sec, Midori and lemon juice over the ice. Shake vigorously until a frost forms.
3 Strain into a chilled cocktail glass.

anouchka

1 measure vodka, iced
dash black Sambuca
dash crème de mure
a few blackberries

SERVES 1

Sambuca is liquorice flavoured and therefore not to everyone's taste. However, used here with a dash of blackberry liqueur and a measure of iced vodka, it's a great combination.

1 Pour the vodka into a chilled shot glass.
2 Add a dash of the Sambuca and then a dash of the crème de mure.
3 Dress with a few blackberries, fresh or frozen.

twin peaks

4–6 cracked ice cubes
dash of Triple Sec
2 measures bourbon
1 measure Bénédictine
1 measure lime juice
slice of lime, to decorate

SERVES 1

Bourbon, named after a county in Kentucky, must be made from at least 51 per cent corn mash and is America's most popular whiskey. It forms the basis of many more cocktails than its Scotch cousin.

1 Put the cracked ice cubes into a cocktail shaker. Dash Triple Sec over the ice and pour in the bourbon, Bénédictine and lime juice. Shake vigorously until a frost forms.
2 Strain into a chilled highball glass and decorate with a slice of lime.

the algonquin

½ measure rye whiskey
½ measure dry vermouth
¼ measure pineapple juice
ice cubes

SERVES 1

Style and sophistication are the key to this drink from the famous Algonquin Hotel in New York.

1 Shake all the ingredients over ice until frosted.
2 Strain into an ice-filled old-fashioned glass.

godfather

4–6 cracked ice cubes
2 measures Scotch whisky
1 measure amaretto

SERVES 1

Amaretto is an Italian liqueur, so perhaps the inspiration for this cocktail comes from Don Corleone, the eponymous character in Mario Puzo's best-selling novel, unforgettably portrayed in the film by Marlon Brando.

1 Fill a chilled highball glass with cracked ice cubes. Pour in the whisky and amaretto and stir to mix.

19th green

1½ measures Irish whiskey
1 measure green Curaçao
ice
dry ginger, to top up

SERVES 1

Whiskey with a kick, perfect for cold wet days and ideal to carry undiluted in a hip flask to help you keep your head down!

1 Stir the whiskey and Curaçao in a tumbler with the ice.
2 Top up with ginger.

dandy

½ measure rye whiskey
½ measure Dubonnet
dash Angostura bitters
3 dashes cassis
ice
few frozen berries,
to decorate

SERVES 1

The fruit flavour added at the end is what gives
this rich combination a special touch.

1 Mix the first four ingredients with ice and
strain into an iced shot glass.
2 Dress with a berry or two.

irish shillelagh

4–6 crushed ice cubes
2 measures Irish whiskey
1 measure lemon juice
½ measure sloe gin
½ measure white rum
½ tsp sugar syrup
½ peach, peeled, stoned and
finely chopped
2 raspberries, to decorate

SERVES 1

A shillelagh (pronounced shee-lay-lee) is a
wooden cudgel, traditionally made from
blackthorn. Undoubtedly, this is a cocktail that
hits the spot.

1 Put the crushed ice cubes into a blender and
add the whiskey, lemon juice, sloe gin, rum,
sugar syrup and chopped peach. Blend until
smooth.
2 Pour into a small, chilled highball glass and
decorate with raspberries.

black watch

⅔ measure Scotch whisky
⅓ measure Kahlúa
or coffee liqueur
ice
soda water, to taste

SERVES 1

An unusual version of whisky and soda that makes a great drink for any time of day or evening.

1 Mix the whisky and liqueur with a few lumps of ice in a large tumbler.
2 Top up with soda water to taste.

mount etna

2 measures whisky
2 measure pure orange juice
shell of ½ lime, squeezed empty
1½ measures Cointreau

SERVES 1

Not surprisingly this is a fairly explosive cocktail. It may not work first time but, if it does, handle with care!

1 Mix the whisky, orange and lime juice in an old-fashioned glass.
2 Soak the lime shell in the Cointreau in a small pan for about 10 minutes.
3 Warm the Cointreau carefully over a low heat. Hold the lime shell in a large spoon, fill it with Cointreau and ignite carefully.
4 Lower immediately into the glass. Allow flames to finish and the glass rim to cool before drinking.

highland fling

4–6 cracked ice cubes
dash of Angostura bitters
2 measures Scotch whisky
1 measure sweet vermouth
cocktail olive, to decorate

SERVES 1

Blended whisky is best suited to cocktails – single malts should always be drunk neat or simply with a little added mineral water. However, a throat-burning, harsh blend will make a mixture closer to rocket fuel than a cocktail and no amount of additional flavours will improve it.

1 Put the cracked ice into a mixing glass.
2 Dash Angostura bitters over the ice. Pour the whisky and vermouth over the ice.
3 Stir well to mix and strain into a chilled glass. Decorate with a cocktail olive.

hayden's milk float

4–6 cracked ice cubes
2 measures white rum
1 measure kirsch
1 measure white crème de cacao
1 measure single cream
grated chocolate,
cocktail cherry, to decorate

SERVES 1

An irresistible melding of perfect partners – rum, cherry, chocolate and cream – this cocktail is almost too good to be true.

1 Put the cracked ice cubes into a cocktail shaker. Pour the rum, kirsch, crème de cacao and cream over the ice. Shake vigorously until a frost forms.
2 Strain into a chilled highball glass. Sprinkle with grated chocolate and decorate with a cocktail cherry.

rum cooler

2 ice cubes
juice of 1 lime
1½ measures rum
1½ measures pineapple juice
1 medium-sized ripe banana,
cut into chunks
lime peel, to decorate

SERVES 1

The characteristic sweetness and perfume of rum blends with so many exotic fruits. You could try this with mango and lychee.

1 Whizz all the ingredients in a blender for about a minute or until smooth.
2 Pour over ice into a chilled glass and finish with a twist of peel.

bishop

4–6 cracked ice cubes
dash of lemon juice
1 measure white rum
1 tsp red wine
pinch of caster sugar

SERVES 1

It is strange how men of the cloth have gained a reputation for being enthusiastic about the good, material things in life. Even Rudyard Kipling wrote about smuggling 'brandy for the parson'. It goes to show that spirituality is no barrier to spirits.

1 Put the cracked ice cubes into a cocktail shaker.
2 Dash the lemon juice over the ice, pour in the white rum and red wine and add a pinch of sugar.
3 Shake vigorously until a frost forms.
4 Strain into a chilled wine glass.

dragon lady

1 measure golden rum
1 measure orange juice
dash white Curaçao
dash grenadine
ice
bitter lemon, chilled, to top up
slice of orange and twist
of peel, to decorate

SERVES 1

The rich fruit flavours of orange, pomegranate
(provided by the grenadine) and lemon,
blended with light rum make a really lovely
long summer drink.

1 Stir the first four ingredients well over ice,
strain into an ice-filled highball glass and top
up with bitter lemon.
2 Add the fruit and top with peel.

yellow bird

1 medium-size ripe pineapple
3 measures dark rum
2 measures Triple Sec
2 measures Galliano
1 measure lime juice
ice cubes
pineapple leaves, to decorate

SERVES 6

This really is best made with fresh sweet ripe pineapple, so you will just have to make a jugful and invite round some friends.

1 Blend the pineapple for 30 seconds in a processor, then add the next four ingredients and blend for another 10–20 seconds until smooth.
2 Pour into large cocktail glasses or tumblers filled with ice and finish with pineapple leaves.

nirvana

8–10 cracked ice cubes
2 measures dark rum
¼ measure grenadine
½ measure tamarind syrup
1 tsp sugar syrup
grapefruit juice, to top up

SERVES 1

It may not be possible to obtain a perfect state of harmony and bliss through a cocktail, but this has to be the next best thing.

1 Put 4–6 cracked ice cubes into a cocktail shaker. Pour the rum, grenadine, tamarind syrup and sugar syrup over the ice and shake vigorously until a frost forms.
2 Half fill a chilled Collins glass with cracked ice cubes and strain the cocktail over them.
3 Top up with grapefruit juice.

dark and stormy

2 measures Mount Gay rum
1 measure lime juice
½ measure sugar syrup
ice
ginger beer, to top up
twist of lime, to decorate

SERVES 1

Golden rum has a mellow, slightly milder taste, but you could use dark rum here for a really stormy mix.

1 Shake the first three ingredients over ice until well frosted.
2 Strain into a chilled highball glass and top up with ginger beer to taste.
3 Dress with a twist of lime.

the bacardi cocktail

2 measures Bacardi rum
2 tsp fresh lime juice
dash grenadine
caster sugar or sugar
syrup, to taste
ice

SERVES 1

White rum, synonymous with the name
Bacardi, is the base of many well-known
cocktails. This one, of course, must be made
with Bacardi.

1 Shake the ingredients over ice until well
frosted.
2 Strain into a shallow cocktail glass.
3 Drink with a straw.

golden galleon

1 measure brandy
1 measure Galliano
1 measure passion fruit juice
dash lemon juice
ice cubes

SERVES 1

The deep yellows of Galliano and passion fruit make sure this cocktail is both a rich golden colour and good fruity flavour.

1 Stir all the ingredients together well in a stirring glass.
2 Strain into an ice-filled tumbler and add a stirrer.

atomic

1¼ measures cognac
¾ measure Grand Marnier
¼ measure blue Curaçao
ice
3 measures exotic
fruit juice, to top up
1 tsp fraise
kiwi slices, to decorate

SERVES 1

Deliciously flavoured with orange and
mandarin, topped up with exotic fruit juices
and decorated with kiwi, this eerie-looking
drink tastes great.

1 Shake the first three ingredients together
over ice until frosted.
2 Strain into a chilled highball glass and top up
with fruit juice.
3 Float in a few drops of fraise and dress with
slices of kiwi.
4 Drink through a straw.

red magic

4–6 cracked ice cubes
dash of Triple Sec
1 measure brandy
1 measure Madeira

SERVES 1

Slowly sip this delightful cocktail and wait for a
pleasantly warm glow to appear in the cockles
of your heart.

1 Put the cracked ice cubes into a mixing glass.
Dash Triple Sec over the ice and pour in the
brandy and Madeira.
2 Stir well to mix, then strain into a chilled
cocktail glass.

fbr

6–8 crushed ice cubes
2 measures brandy
1½ measures white rum
1 tbsp lemon juice
1 tsp sugar syrup
1 egg white

SERVES 1

A number of cocktails are known simply by initials. In this case, FBR stands for Frozen Brandy and Rum. Others seem to be quite obscure and, in one or two instances, slightly naughty.

1 Put the crushed ice, brandy, rum, lemon juice, sugar syrup and egg white into a blender.
2 Blend until slushy and pour into a chilled highball glass.

american beauty

1 measure brandy
1 measure dry vermouth
1 measure grenadine
1 measure orange juice
1 dash white crème de menthe
ice
2–3 dashes port

SERVES 1

This sumptuous drink packs quite a punch, so beware of too many beauties – appreciate them slowly.

1 Shake all the ingredients, except the port, together over ice until well frosted.
2 Strain into a chilled cocktail glass and gently add the port so that it floats on top.

triple champion

1 measure Cinzano bianco
1 measure Triple Sec
1–2 measures pink or ruby
grapefruit juice
½ measure ruby port
ice

SERVES 1

Pink or ruby grapefruit juices are sweeter and gentler flavours than classic white grapefruit juices, so are very good mixers in cocktails.

1 Mix all the ingredients in a tall tumbler with ice.

raffles

1 measure white vermouth
¼ measure gin
¼ measure Campari
ice
slice of orange, to decorate

SERVES 1

A popular cocktail from colonial days, before tonic stole the show.

1 Stir the ingredients over ice in a chilled medium tumbler.
2 Squeeze in a slice of orange and leave it in the glass.

americano

1 measure Campari
1 measure sweet vermouth
ice
soda water, to top up
twist of orange or lemon
peel, to decorate

SERVES 1

A light refreshing cocktail for lovers of the bitter-sweet Campari, easy anytime drinking to make as strong or weak as you like.

1 Pour the Campari and vermouth into a highball glass filled with ice.
2 Stir well and then top up with soda water.
3 Dress with a twist of orange or lemon peel.

teaser

1 measure tequila
1 measure orange liqueur
1 measure fresh lime juice
1 dash egg white
ice
lime slice or twist, to decorate

SERVES 1

Don't be tempted into thinking this looks like a refreshing glass of frosted juice!

1 Shake all the ingredients, except the lime slice, together over ice until frosted.
2 Pour into a chilled cocktail glass and finish with a twist or slice of lime and an ice cube.

huatusco whammer

8–10 cracked ice cubes
1 measure white tequila
½ measure white rum
½ measure vodka
½ measure gin
½ measure Triple Sec
1 measure lemon juice
½ tsp sugar syrup
cola, to top up

SERVES 1

To be authentic, this cocktail should be topped up with Coca-Cola, but you can use other brands of cola if you prefer. Make sure that the cola is well chilled before adding it.

1 Put 4–6 cracked ice cubes into a cocktail shaker.
2 Pour the tequila, rum, vodka, gin, Triple Sec, lemon juice and sugar syrup over the ice. Shake vigorously until a frost forms.
3 Fill a chilled Collins glass with cracked ice cubes and strain the cocktail over them. Top up with cola, stir gently and serve with straws.

carolina

4–6 cracked ice cubes
3 measures golden tequila
1 tsp grenadine
1 tsp vanilla essence
1 measure single cream
1 egg white
ground cinnamon,
cocktail cherry, to decorate

SERVES 1

White tequila is most commonly used for mixing cocktails, but some require the mellower flavour of the amber-coloured, aged tequilas, which are known as golden tequila or añejo.

1 Put the cracked ice cubes into a cocktail shaker.
2 Pour the tequila, grenadine, vanilla and cream over the ice and add the egg white. Shake vigorously until a frost forms.
3 Strain into a chilled cocktail glass. Sprinkle with cinnamon and decorate with a cocktail cherry.

tequila steeler

1 measure tequila
½ measure white rum
½ measure vodka
¼ measure coconut cream
dash lime juice
few drops grenadine
ice
flower or petals
strips of lime peel,
to decorate

SERVES 1

Rich creamy coconut helps to smooth this fiery combination, but don't be fooled by the soft baby pink colour!

1 Shake the first six ingredients well together over ice.
2 Pour into a chilled glass and finish with a flower or petals and a strip of lime peel.

el diablo

6–8 cracked ice cubes
2–3 strips of lime peel
1 measure lime juice
3 measures white tequila
1 measure crème de cassis

SERVES 1

One or two Diablos and you will certainly feel a bit of a devil, but one or two too many and you will feel like the very devil!

1 Fill a small, chilled glass with cracked ice cubes and add the lime peel.
2 Pour the lime juice over the ice and add the tequila and crème de cassis.

tequila mockingbird

4–6 cracked ice cubes
2 measures white tequila
1 measure white crème de menthe
1 measure fresh lime juice

SERVES 1

In spite of the horrible literary pun in the name, this popular cocktail is fast becoming a modern classic.

1 Put the cracked ice cubes into a cocktail shaker. Add the tequila, crème de menthe and lime juice. Shake vigorously until a frost forms.
2 Strain into a chilled highball glass.

coco loco

1 fresh coconut
8–10 crushed ice cubes
2 measures white tequila
1 measure gin
1 measure white rum
2 measures pineapple juice
1 tsp sugar syrup
½ lime

SERVES 1

This is a truly spectacular cocktail and can be great fun to decorate. Look out for swizzle sticks in the shape of palm trees or hula dancers and elaborately curly straws.

1 Carefully saw the top off the coconut, reserving the liquid inside.
2 Add the crushed ice, tequila, gin, rum, pineapple juice and sugar syrup to the coconut, together with the reserved coconut liquid.
3 Squeeze the lime over the cocktail and drop it in. Stir well and serve with a straw.

bombshell

1 measure tequila
2 measures dry Marsala
splash Campari
splash cherry brandy
piece of lemon, to decorate

SERVES 1

Tequila will give any cocktail a good kick, but this concoction is really not as strong as its name implies!

1 Mix the ingredients straight into a small tumbler or cocktail glass with ice.
2 Finish with a piece of lemon.

adonis

1 measure sherry
½ measure red vermouth
ice
dash orange bitters
orange peel, to decorate

SERVES 1

The sherry you choose makes all the difference to this drink, be it dry, sweet or the slightly nutty medium-sweet amontillado

1 Stir the ingredients over ice in a chilled medium tumbler.
2 Dress with the orange peel.

which way?

4–6 cracked ice cubes
1 measure Pernod
1 measure Anisette
1 measure brandy

SERVES 1

Aniseed-flavoured pastis, such as Pernod, are firm favourites in today's cocktail bars and often form the basis of almost lethally strong drinks.

1 Put the cracked ice cubes into a cocktail shaker.
2 Pour the Pernod, Anisette and brandy over the ice. Shake vigorously until a frost forms.
3 Strain into a chilled wine glass.

watermelon man

4 measures dry white wine
1 dash grenadine
scoop crushed ice
4 cubes or chunks of
watermelon, to decorate

Watermelon is such a colourful and tasty fruit that it makes a great mixer. Don't be tempted to add more unless you want to dilute the strength of your cocktail.

SERVES 1

1 Whizz all the ingredients together in a blender for 5–10 seconds until well frosted.
2 Pour into a tall glass and dress with a piece of melon on a cocktail stick.

sparkling cocktails

french 75

4–6 cracked ice cubes
2 measures brandy
1 measure lemon juice
1 tbsp sugar syrup
champagne, chilled
twist of lemon peel,
to decorate

SERVES 1

Described in a cocktail book of the early 20th century as a drink that 'definitely hits the spot', there seems to be some confusion about the actual ingredients for this classic. All recipes include champagne, but disagree about the spirits included.

1 Put the cracked ice cubes into a cocktail shaker.
2 Pour the brandy, lemon juice and sugar syrup over the ice and shake vigorously until a frost forms.
3 Strain into a chilled highball glass and top up with champagne. Decorate with the lemon twist.

champagne cocktail

1 sugar cube
2 dashes Angostura bitters
1 measure brandy
champagne, chilled

SERVES 1

The classic champagne cocktail can be too sweet for some. It is the brandy that gives the treat and the kick, so you could leave out the sugar!

1 Place the sugar cube with the drops of bitters in the base of a chilled flute.
2 Pour on the brandy and top up slowly with champagne.

jade

4–6 cracked ice cubes
dash of Angostura bitters
¼ measure Midori
¼ measure blue Curaçao
¼ measure lime juice
champagne, chilled
slice of lime, to decorate

SERVES 1

You can tell good jade because it always feel cold to the touch – and that should apply to cocktails, too. No cocktail bar – whether in a hotel, pub or at home – can ever have too much ice.

1 Put the cracked ice cubes into a cocktail shaker. Dash Angostura bitters over the ice and pour in the Midori, Curaçao and lime juice. Shake vigorously until a frost forms.
2 Strain into a chilled champagne flute. Top up with chilled champagne and decorate with a slice of lime.

campari fizz

1 measure Campari
1 measure orange juice
crushed ice
champagne, chilled

SERVES 1

The bitter-sweet taste of Campari is a natural with orange juice and sparkling wine or champagne. You need very little Campari to add the distinctive colour and flavour.

1 Shake the first three ingredients together well until frosted and pour into a flute.
2 Top up with champagne.

buck's fizz

2 measures champagne, chilled
2 measures orange juice, chilled

SERVES 1

Invented at Buck's Club in London, the original was invariably made with Bollinger champagne and it is true that the better the quality of the champagne, the better the flavour.

1 Pour the champagne into a chilled champagne flute, then pour in the orange juice.

champagne cobbler

1 glass champagne, chilled
¼ measure Curaçao
1 tsp syrup de gomme
ice
raspberry and soft fruit slices,
to decorate

SERVES 1

The Cobbler was popular in Dickens' time when it was a concoction of sherry, sugar, lemon and ice. This version has much more kick and lots more bubbles.

1 Mix the champagne, Curaçao and syrup in a chilled mixing glass.
2 Pour into a tall glass filled with ice and simply dress with pieces of fresh soft fruit.

the footman

½ measure gin
1 measure orange juice
1 slice peach
1 ice cube
champagne, chilled
1 slice of peach, to decorate

SERVES 1

If you are preparing several glasses, make the gin base in advance and keep it well chilled until you are ready.

1 Whizz all except the champagne in a blender until smooth, about 10 seconds.
2 Pour into a flute and top up with champagne when ready.
3 Finish with a slice of peach.

pear and cinnamon sling

2 measures vodka
2 measure pear purée
¾ measure cinnamon syrup
⅙ measure cranberry and blackcurrant juice
ice
champagne, chilled
slices of pear, to decorate

SERVES 1

If you can't find cinnamon syrup, you may have to make your own!

1 Shake the first four ingredients together over ice until frosted.
2 Strain into a chilled flute and top up with champagne.
3 Dress with pear.

san remo

½ measure grapefruit juice
¼ measure Triple Sec
¼ measure mandarin liqueur
ice
champagne, chilled
slices of frozen citrus fruit,
to decorate

SERVES 1

Next time you cut up a citrus fruit, put any left-over slices in the freezer, as they make great flavoured ice cubes.

1 Mix the first three ingredients with ice in a tall glass.
2 Top up with champagne and dress with fruit.

alfonso

1 measure Dubonnet
1 sugar cube
2 dashes Angostura bitters
champagne or sparkling
wine, chilled
orange peel, to decorate

SERVES 1

This is a delicious way to turn a simple sparkling white wine into a sophisticated cocktail. Probably not the time to use expensive champagne.

1 Pour the Dubonnet into a chilled flute.
2 Add the sugar lump with the bitters splashed onto it.
3 When ready to serve, pour on the chilled bubbly and add a twist of orange peel.

caribbean champagne

½ measure white rum
½ measure crème de banane
champagne, chilled
slice of banana, to decorate

SERVES 1

Both rum and bananas are naturally associated with the Tropics, but wine does not spring so readily to mind when the Caribbean is mentioned. However, remember that France shares a long history with many of the Caribbean islands, such as Martinique and Guadeloupe.

1 Pour the rum and crème de banane into a chilled flute.
2 Top up with champagne.
3 Stir gently to mix, and dress with a slice of banana.

josiah's bay float

cracked ice cubes
2 measures golden rum
1 measure Galliano
2 measures pineapple juice
1 measure lime juice
4 tsp sugar syrup
champagne, to top up
scooped-out pineapple shell
slices of lime and lemon,
cocktail cherries, to decorate

SERVES 2

This is a wonderful cocktail for a special
occasion in the summer. Designed for two to
share, perhaps an engagement or a romantic al
fresco dinner would be appropriate. For the
more prosaic, serve in tall, chilled tumblers,
rather than a pineapple shell.

1 Shake the rum, Galliano, pineapple juice,
lime juice and sugar syrup vigorously over ice
until well frosted.
2 Strain into the pineapple shell, top up with
champagne and stir gently.
3 Decorate with lime and lemon slices and
cocktail cherries and serve with two straws.

sparkling gold

1 measure golden rum
½ measure Cointreau
champagne, chilled

SERVES 1

For a very special occasion like a golden wedding anniversary, you could float tiny pieces of edible gold leaf on the top of each glass.

1 Pour the rum and liqueur into a chilled flute and top up with chilled champagne.

christmas cocktail

1 cube sugar
splash brandy
generous splash
cranberry juice, chilled
champagne, chilled
few raspberries, to decorate

SERVES 1

This bright and cheerful cocktail is easy to prepare for lots of guests and you certainly don't need to wait for Christmas to enjoy it.

1 Place a sugar cube in the base of a chilled champagne glass.
2 Add the brandy and allow to soak in, then splash on the cranberry juice.
3 At the last moment, top up with champagne and float one or two raspberries on the top.

kismet

1 measure gin
1 measure apricot brandy
½ tsp stem ginger syrup
champagne, chilled
slices of ripe fresh mango,
to decorate

SERVES 1

A romantic era produced some delightful music
and this elegant drink brings that mood bang
up to date.

1 Pour the gin and brandy into a chilled flute.
2 Trickle the ginger syrup slowly down the
glass and then top up with champagne.
3 Add a piece of fruit to finish.

the bentley

½ measure cognac or brandy
½ measure peach liqueur, peach brandy or schnapps
juice of 1 passion fruit, sieved
1 ice cube
champagne, chilled

SERVES 1

Champagne cocktails tend to get better and better the more you drink.

1 Mix the first three ingredients gently together in a chilled glass.
2 Add one ice cube and slowly pour in champagne to taste.

chicago

egg white or lemon juice
caster sugar
1 measure brandy
1 dash Cointreau
1 dash Angostura bitters
ice
champagne, chilled

SERVES 1

Do use a dry champagne, or even a good sparkling wine, for cocktails where you add sweet ingredients and especially if you want to sugar the rim of the glass for extra sparkle.

1 Prepare a frosted rim glass with the egg white and sugar.
2 Shake the rest of the ingredients together (except the champagne) with ice until frosted.
3 Strain into the prepared glass and top up with champagne.

dawn

1 measure lime juice
1 measure medium to medium dry sherry
champagne, chilled

SERVES 1

If you don't have any champagne available, then look for a good fruity sparkling white wine, or even a sparkling red, to use in this cocktail.

1 Stir the lime and sherry in a chilled flute.
2 Top with chilled champagne and stir briefly.

royal julep

1 sugar lump
3 sprigs fresh mint
1 measure Jack Daniels
champagne, chilled

SERVES 1

As with all juleps, the mint needs crushing or muddling first to help release its flavour into the sugar and water. Simply chopping it won't produce enough flavour.

1 In a small glass, crush the sugar and mint together with a little of the whiskey.
2 When the sugar has dissolved, strain it into a chilled flute with the rest of the whiskey and then top up with champagne.

pick-me-up

ice
3 dashes Fernet Branca
3 dashes Curaçao
1 measure brandy
champagne, chilled
lemon peel, to decorate

SERVES 1

Champagne always gives you a lift and this one, with its added ingredients, is the perfect anytime booster.

1 Place the ice in a wine glass to chill.
2 Stir in the other ingredients gradually and top up with the champagne.
3 Dress with a twist of lemon peel.

lady luck

1 measure Calvados
1 measure pear nectar or
½ measure pear liqueur
slice of firm ripe pear,
to decorate
champagne, chilled

SERVES 1

The pear and apple flavours give a deep fruitiness to the final cocktail, so you could equally well use a sparkling white wine as the base.

1 Pour the Calvados and pear nectar or liqueur into a chilled flute with a slice of pear.
2 Top up with chilled champagne.

bombay sherry punch

1 bottle brandy, chilled
1 bottle sherry, chilled
1 measure maraschino
1 measure Curaçao
2 bottles champagne or
sparkling white wine, chilled
soda water, chilled
large ice cubes
(set with fruit in them)
fruit, to decorate

SERVES 16

An unusual mix for a party, ideal to dilute as much as you wish.

1 Mix the first four ingredients in a large punch bowl.
2 Add the champagne or wine and soda to taste and then add the fruit and ice cubes at the last minute.

wild silk

½ measure cream
½ measure raspberries
1 measure framboise or
raspberry syrup
little crushed ice
champagne, chilled

A wildly fruity cocktail topped with a riot of
bubbles and really well-iced champagne.

1 Set aside 2–3 nice raspberries.
2 Whizz the first three ingredients with ice in a
blender until frosted and slushy.
3 Pour into a flute and top up with champagne.
Float a raspberry or two on the top.

black velvet

stout or Guinness, chilled
champagne, chilled

SERVES 1

Don't ever say that it ruins good champagne, just
enjoy a long heady draught of a timeless
treasure.

1 Pour both drinks in equal quantities carefully
(may fizz up well) into a long beer or highball
glass.

the trade winds

1 measure gin
½ measure cherry brandy
½ measure lemon juice
1–2 dashes syrup de gomme
½ scoop crushed ice
champagne, chilled
cherries, to decorate

SERVES 1

Whether it blows hot or cold, champagne cocktails are a treat for any occasion and this one is as refreshing as it is colourful.

1 Shake together all but the champagne over ice until frosted and strain into the base of a champagne glass.
2 Top up with chilled champagne and decorate with fresh cherries.

serpentine

½ measure green
crème de menthe
cracked ice
curl or twist of lime peel
champagne, chilled
1 tsp lime zest, to decorate

SERVES 1

Living up to its name, this green bubbly
concoction has hidden secrets. Don't forget to
chill the champagne for at least two hours
before mixing.

1 Pour the crème de menthe into the base of a
flute with ice and the curl of lime peel.
2 Pour in the champagne and finish with a
sprinkle of zest.

monte carlo

½ measure gin
¼ measure lemon juice
ice
champagne or sparkling
white wine, chilled
¼ measure crème de menthe
mint leaf, to decorate

SERVES 1

The motor racing world always drinks champagne, especially in Monte Carlo, and this well-laced cocktail is definitely a Formula 1 special.

1 Stir the first two ingredients over ice until well chilled.
2 Strain into chilled flutes and top up with champagne.
3 Finally drizzle the crème de menthe over the top and dress with a mint leaf.

prince of wales

1 measure brandy
1 measure Madeira wine or
muscatel
3 drops Curaçao
2 drops Angostura bitters
ice
champagne, chilled
orange peel, to decorate

SERVES 1

A knockout version of a champagne cocktail, not to be drunk too quickly.

1 Shake the first four ingredients together over ice and strain into a chilled flute.
2 Top up with champagne to taste and finish with a fine curl of orange peel.

long tall sally

¼ measure brandy
¼ measure dry vermouth
¼ measure Galliano
¼ measure mandarin
liqueur
ice
champagne or
sparkling wine, chilled

SERVES 1

A seriously strong champagne cocktail with the perfume of herbs.

1 Stir the first four ingredients over ice and pour into a tall chilled glass.
2 Top up with champagne.

kir royale

few drops cassis or to taste
½ measure brandy
champagne, chilled

SERVES 1

A wicked improvement on the simple cassis
and white wine drink.

1 Put the cassis and brandy into the base of a
flute.
2 Top up with champagne to taste.

james bond

1 sugar cube
2 dashes Angostura bitters
1 measure vodka, chilled
champagne, chilled

SERVES 1

Surprisingly and very definitely not shaken on this occasion, or stirred!

1 Moisten the sugar with the Angostura and place in the base of a chilled flute.
2 Cover with the vodka and then top up with champagne.

grape expectations

5–6 red or black grapes
ice
splash of mandarin liqueur
pink champagne or sparkling
wine, chilled

SERVES 1

Add the remaining grapes at the very last minute, then watch them liven up your drink as they jump around, making ever more bubbles.

1 Save two grapes for the glass.
2 Crush or muddle the others in a small bowl to let the juice flow.
3 Add ice and liqueur, stir well and strain into a chilled champagne glass.
4 Top up with champagne. Halve and pip the remaining grapes and add to the glass.

mimosa

juice of 1 passion fruit
½ measure orange Curaçao
crushed ice
champagne, chilled
slice of star fruit and twist
of peel, to decorate

SERVES 1

So called because it resembles the colour of a mimosa's attractive yellow bloom.

1 Scoop out the passion fruit flesh into a jug or shaker and shake with the Curaçao and a little crushed ice until frosted.
2 Pour into the base of a champagne glass and top up with champagne.
3 Dress with fruit.

sparkling julep

1 lump sugar
2 sprigs mint
sparkling white wine, chilled
fruit, to decorate

SERVES 1

Sparkling wine is good to enjoy any time and this is a particularly refreshing way to drink it.

1 Place the sugar in the base of a chilled flute with one bruised sprig of mint.
2 Add the bubbly and the other sprig of mint and any fruit in season you wish.

day dreamer

⅓ measure brandy
1 tsp maraschino
1 tsp dark Curaçao
1 tsp Angostura bitters
ice
champagne or sparkling
white wine, chilled
fresh cherry, to decorate

SERVES 1

You won't need more than one of these before you are daydreaming.

1 Stir the first four ingredients over ice, strain into a cocktail glass and top up with champagne.
2 Dress with a cherry.

tequila slammer

1 measure white
tequila
1 measure lemon juice
sparkling wine,
chilled, to top up

SERVES 1

Slammers, also known as shooters, are currently very fashionable. The idea is that you pour the different ingredients directly into the glass, without stirring (some slammers form colourful layers). Cover the top of the glass with one hand to prevent spillage, then slam the glass on the bar or a table to mix and drink the cocktail down in one. It is essential to use a strong glass that is unlikely to break under such treatment.

1 Put the tequila and lemon juice into a chilled glass and stir to mix. Top up with sparkling wine.
2 Cover the glass with your hand and slam.

sabrina

½ measure gin
⅛ measure apricot brandy
½ measure fresh orange juice
1 tsp grenadine
¼ measure Cinzano
ice
sweet sparkling wine, chilled
orange and lemon slices,
to decorate

SERVES 1

Perfect for lovers of sweet and fruity cocktails, and the base is easy to prepare in advance.

1 Shake the first five ingredients together over ice.
2 Pour into a tall glass and top up with sparkling wine.
3 Finish with slices of orange and lemon.

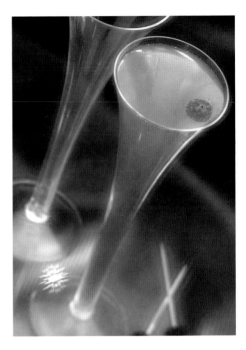

black sparkler

1¾ measures cognac
¼ measure Crème de Mure
¼ measure lemon juice
1 tsp caster sugar
ice
soda water or
sparkling white wine, chilled
frozen blackcurrants or berries,
to decorate

SERVES 1

Simply using sparkling water makes this a delicious summer party drink. If you wish to make it more celebratory, use sparkling white wine.

1 Shake the first four ingredients over ice until frosted.
2 Strain into a tall chilled cocktail glass and top up with soda water or wine.
3 Dress with fruit.

velvet mule

1 measure cassis
1 measure black Sambuca
2 measures ginger wine
cola
soda or sparkling white wine,
chilled

SERVES 1

This mule has an interesting kick of anise and ginger – a surprisingly good mix, especially with unique flavours from the cola.

1 Stir the first three ingredients over ice until well frosted.
2 Strain into a frosted flute and top up with equal quantities of cola and soda or sparkling wine.

orange sparkler

⅔ measure brandy
⅓ measure orange liqueur
⅓ measure lemon juice
ice
sparkling dry white wine,
chilled

SERVES 1

Serve this exotic version of a classic champagne cocktail for any occasion or simple celebration.

1 Shake the first three ingredients well together over ice.
2 Strain into a chilled champagne glass and top up with sparkling wine to taste.

amarettine

⅓ measure Amaretto
⅓ measure dry vermouth
sparkling white wine, chilled

SERVES 1

Inexpensive sparkling white wine is the base of this pretty cocktail. Use the sweeter bubblies if you like a sweet drink, otherwise go for dry. And be warned, it is not just a pretty drink!

1 Mix the Amaretto and vermouth in a chilled tall cocktail glass.
2 Top up with wine to taste.

san joaquin punch

1 tbsp raisins or chopped prunes
6 tsp brandy
300ml/10 fl oz sparkling white wine or champagne, chilled
300m/l10 fl oz white cranberry and grape juice
ice

SERVES 4

A fabulous bubbly punch enriched with brandy-soaked Californian dried fruits.

1 Mix the dried fruit and brandy in a small bowl and leave to soak for 1–2 hours.
2 In a jug, mix the sparkling wine, juice and brandy-soaked fruit.
3 Pour into ice-filled glasses.

raspberry mist

6 measures Irish Mist honey
liqueur
450g/1lb raspberries
crushed ice
4 bottles sparkling dry white
wine, well chilled
24 raspberries, to decorate

SERVES 24

The perfect celebration drink for a ruby
wedding anniversary.

1 Whiz the liqueur and raspberries in a blender
with a cup of crushed ice.
2 When lightly frozen, divide between chilled
champagne bowls and top up with the wine.
3 Top each with a raspberry.

disco dancer

1 measure crème de banane
1 measure rum
few drops Angostura bitters
ice
sparkling white wine, chilled

SERVES 1

Make it nice and long and you have the perfect
disco drink.

1 Shake all the first three ingredients well over
ice.
2 Pour into a high ball glass and top up with
sparkling wine to taste.
3 Add plenty of ice to keep you cool and
lengthen your drink.

pink sherbet royale

300ml/10 fl oz sparkling
white wine, chilled
2 measures cassis
1 measure brandy
1 scoop crushed ice
blackberries, to decorate

SERVES 2

This is perfect for very special occasions on hot
days, or after dinner watching a warm sun
setting slowly.

1 Whizz half the wine in a blender with the rest
of the ingredients until really frothy and frosted
(mind it doesn't bubble over).
2 Slowly whisk in a little more wine and pour
into tall thin frosted glasses.
3 Top with a few blackberries.

shangri-la

½ measure gin
¼ measure apricot brandy
½ measure orange juice
few drops grenadine
ice
dry sparkling white wine,
chilled
slices of orange and lemon,
to decorate

SERVES 1

This an excellent mix to liven up a not-so-exciting bottle of bubbly! Also an unusual mix for several people for a party.

1 Stir the first four ingredients with ice in a chilled highball or large wine glass.
2 Top up with sparkling wine and dress with fruit.

cider punch

500ml/17 fl oz dry sparkling
cider
150ml/5 fl oz cognac or brandy
150ml/5 fl oz Cointreau
ice
apple slices, to decorate
300ml/10 fl oz soda water
or dry ginger

SERVES 10

This may sound seriously strong but it isn't, and
you can add more soda or ice to taste once the
base is made.

1 Mix the first three ingredients together and
chill in the refrigerator until required.
2 Pour into a large punch bowl with ice, apple
slices and the soda water or dry ginger.
3 Serve in small cups or glasses.

apple fizz

150ml/5 fl oz sparkling cider or
apple juice
1 measure Calvados
juice of half a lemon
1 tbsp egg white
generous pinch sugar
ice
slices of lemon and apple,
to decorate

SERVES 1

Cider makes a great punch base, as it can be blended with many alcoholic drinks. This mix can't be made in advance, but it's easy to prepare for several people and then add more cider at the last minute to create extra fizz.

1 Shake the first five ingredients together over ice and pour immediately into a highball glass (it may fizz up well).
2 Finish with a slice of lemon or apple or both. For more fizz at the last moment, top up with more cider.

mexican fizz

2 measures tequila
½ measure grenadine
5–6 measures dry ginger ale
crushed ice

SERVES 1

The tart fruitiness of tequila is not often appreciated neat, but it is great with many of the sweetened and fuller flavoured mixers.

1 Shake the tequila, grenadine and half the ginger ale over ice until slushy and frosted.
2 Pour into a chilled tall glass and top up with more ginger ale to taste.
3 Drink through a straw.

peardrops

1 measure pear schnapps
perry, chilled
slice of pear or a cherry,
to decorate

SERVES 1

Pear is one fruit that adds an alcoholic type of
flavour, whether it is in alcohol form or not.
When you cook pears, they become more
aromatic and in this cocktail they certainly give
off a wonderfully rich and heady aroma.

1 Pour the schnapps into the base of a chilled
champagne glass and slowly add the perry.
2 Dress with a cherry.

liqueur cocktails

panda

4–6 cracked ice cubes
dash of sugar syrup
1 measure slivovitz
1 measure apple brandy
1 measure gin
1 measure orange juice

SERVES 1

Slivovitz is a colourless plum brandy, usually made from Mirabelle and Switzen plums. It is usually drunk straight, but can add a fruity note to cocktails. If it is not available, you could substitute apricot, peach or cherry brandy – all fruits from the same family – but the cocktail will not look or taste quite the same.

1 Put the cracked ice cubes into a cocktail shaker.
2 Dash the sugar syrup over the ice and pour in the slivovitz, apple brandy, gin and orange juice. Shake vigorously until a frost forms.
3 Strain into a chilled cocktail glass.

honeymoon

8–10 cracked ice cubes
4 measures apple brandy
2 measures Bénédictine
2 measures lemon juice
2 tsp Triple Sec

SERVES 2

The traditional nuptial journey is so called because the first month of marriage was thought to be sweet – and why not? If you are sick of the sight of champagne following the wedding, why not share this sweet concoction?

1 Put the cracked ice cubes into a cocktail shaker.
2 Pour the brandy, Bénédictine, lemon juice and Triple Sec over the ice. Shake vigorously until a frost forms.
3 Strain into two chilled cocktail glasses.

indian summer

1 measure vodka
2 measures Kahlúa
1 measure gin
2 measures pineapple juice
ice
tonic water

SERVES 1

The coffee liqueur is the key ingredient in this delicious long mix – it would be good with crème de noyeau or crème de cacao too.

1 Shake the first four ingredients well over ice until frosted.
2 Strain into a medium cocktail glass or wine glass and top up with tonic water to taste.

on the vine

½ measure apricot brandy
ice
dash grenadine
150ml/5 fl oz white wine
or to taste
soda water
small bunch grapes, to decorate

SERVES 1

The wine you use in this cocktail can change the character of the mix totally. If you like a sweet drink, use a medium sweet or sweet wine. Otherwise, choose a dry or drier wine.

1 Stir the apricot brandy and ice in a large cocktail glass or wine goblet.
2 Add the grenadine and then pour on the wine.
3 Top up with soda for a longer, more refreshing drink.
4 Dress the glass with grapes.

kokoloko

cocoa powder
caster sugar
1 measure coconut cream
1 measure coconut rum
1 measure crème de cacao
1 measure milk
ice

SERVES 1

For a stunning party effect, quickly dip the rim of the glass first in one of the liqueurs, then into a mixture of cocoa and caster sugar.

1 Frost the rim of the glass using a little liqueur, cocoa powder and sugar.
Set aside to dry.
2 Mix the first four ingredients together and pour over ice in a tumbler.

millionaire

⅔ measure apricot brandy
⅔ measure sloe gin
⅔ measure Jamaican rum
dash grenadine
juice ½ lemon or lime
ice
few blueberries, to decorate

SERVES 1

There are many versions of this cocktail, mainly dependent on the unusual contents of your cocktail cabinet.

1 Shake all the ingredients except the berries well over ice and strain into an ice-filled cocktail glass.
2 Add a few blueberries at the last minute.

grasshopper

2 measures green
crème de menthe
2 measures white
crème de cacao
2 measures single cream
4–6 cracked ice cubes

SERVES 1

Experts disagree on this original recipe and
there seem to be at least three versions with
the same name – as well as numerous
variations. The recipe given here is also known
as a Grasshopper Surprise.

1 Shake the crème de menthe, crème de cacao
and single cream over ice until a frost forms.
2 Strain into a chilled goblet.

jealousy

1 tsp crème de menthe
1–2 tbsp double cream
2 measures coffee or
chocolate liqueur
crushed ice
chocolate matchsticks

SERVES 1

This really is an after-dinner cocktail and if you want a change, you could occasionally flavour the cream with a different liqueur.

1 Gently beat the mint liqueur into the cream until thick.
2 Pour the coffee liqueur into a very small iced cocktail glass and carefully spoon on the whipped flavoured cream.
3 Serve with chocolate matchsticks.

last tango

2–3 thin slices ripe mango,
part-frozen, to decorate
1½ measures Mandarine
Napoleon
½ measure kirsch
crushed ice

SERVES 1

Use the mango slices here as added ice cubes.
They look and taste great and do a good job.

1 Put the thin slices of peeled mango into the
freezer 40–50 minutes before you need them.
2 Shake the liqueurs well over ice until frosted.
Pour into a chilled cocktail glass and add the
slices of mango.

minted diamonds

1 tsp green crème de menthe
1 tbsp iced water
1 measure white
crème de menthe
2 measures apple or
pear schnapps
ice

SERVES 1

Make these stunning ice cubes well in advance
and only take out of the freezer at the very last
second – they melt almost immediately.

1 Mix the green crème de menthe with 1 tbsp
iced water and freeze in 1 or 2 small ice cubes
for about two hours.
2 Stir the other liqueurs over ice until well
frosted.
3 Strain into a chilled cocktail glass and float the
mint ice cubes on top at the last moment.
4 Don't start drinking until the mint cubes begin
to melt!

hazy lady

½ measure crème de noyeau
½ measure coffee liqueur
½ measure brandy
½ measure orange juice
dash egg white
dash grenadine
grated nutmeg, to decorate

SERVES 1

The bright pink grenadine soon trickles through these rich nutty flavoured liqueurs to give a pretty base layer.

1 Shake the first five ingredients together over ice until frosted.
2 Strain into an iced cocktail glass and dress with a dash of grenadine and sprinkling of nutmeg.

knuckle duster

1 measure coconut liqueur
1 measure blue Curaçao
½ measure white rum
¼ measure pineapple juice
crushed ice
toasted shredded coconut,
to decorate

SERVES 1

Just sip quietly and your blues will soon drift away...

1 Whizz the first five ingredients together in a blender until frothy and partly frozen.
2 Pour into a tall iced glass, top up with more ice and finish with a little toasted shredded coconut.

nuclear fallout

1 tsp raspberry syrup
¼ measure of maraschino
¼ measure of yellow
Chartreuse
¼ measure Cointreau
½ measure well-iced blue
Curaçao

SERVES 1

This is similar to a pousse-café, where the liqueurs are layered, but, in this case, the heaviest liqueur is coldest and is added last, to create the slow sinking effect!

1 Chill all the liqueurs, but specifically put the blue Curaçao in the coldest part of the freezer. Also chill a shot, pousse-café or elgin glass.
2 Carefully pour the first four ingredients one by one in layers over the back of a teaspoon.
3 Finally, pour in the blue Curaçao and wait for the fallout!

adam's apple

4–6 cracked ice cubes
dash of yellow Chartreuse
2 measures apple brandy
1 measure gin
1 measure dry vermouth

SERVES 1

Applejack in the United States, Calvados in France and apple brandy as a generic term – whatever you call it, it provides a delicious fruity flavour and a tempting aroma to this cocktail.

1 Put the cracked ice cubes into a mixing glass.
2 Dash the Chartreuse over the ice and pour in the apple brandy, gin and vermouth.
3 Stir well to mix, then strain into a chilled glass.

mexican dawn

1 measure coconut liqueur
1 measure tequila
1 scoop strawberry ice cream
dash strawberry liqueur
dash tamarind syrup
flake or piece of fresh
coconut, to decorate

SERVES 1

Creamy and richly flavoured with a hint of
daring, just like Mexico.

1 Whizz all the ingredients except the coconut
in a blender slowly for about 10 seconds.
2 Pour into a chilled cocktail glass and decorate
with a flake of fresh or candied coconut. Serve
with a stirrer.

banana cocktail

1 measure advocaat
1 measure crème de banane
1 ripe banana
wine glass crushed ice
soda water, to top up

SERVES 1

This can be quite sweet and rich so enough ice and the right touch of soda water are important.

1 Whizz all except the soda in a blender until smooth and well frosted.
2 Pour into a chilled highball glass and top up with soda water to taste.

jack frost

¾ measure blue Curaçao,
chilled
caster sugar
1 measure tequila, chilled
2 measures cream, chilled
½ cup crushed ice

SERVES 1

It looks dramatic and icy cold, but it tastes
delicious and has enough kick to warm you up
despite the cool blue.

1 Dip the rim of a medium size cocktail glass in
the Curaçao, shake off any excess and dip
immediately into caster sugar.
2 Set aside in a cold place to dry and set.
3 Shake the rest of the ingredients and the
Curaçao over ice until really frosted.
4 Pour carefully into the glass.

pink squirrel

4–6 cracked ice cubes
2 measures dark
crème de cacao
1 measure crème de noyaux
1 measure single cream

SERVES 1

Crème de noyaux has a wonderful, slightly bitter,
nutty flavour, but is, in fact, made from peach
and apricot kernels. It is usually served as a
liqueur, but does combine well with some other
ingredients in cocktails.

1 Put the cracked ice cubes into a cocktail
shaker.
2 Pour the crème de cacao, crème de noyaux
and single cream over the ice. Shake vigorously
until a frost forms.
3 Strain into a chilled cocktail glass.

adam'n'eve

2 measures Triple Sec
1 measure vodka
1 measure grapefruit juice
1 measure cranberry juice
ice
5–6 cubes pineapple
2 tsp caster sugar
crushed ice
strawberry, to decorate

SERVES 1

Don't expect this cocktail to be full of apples!
The base is sharp and astringent, while the top
is sweet and frothy – no discrimination here, of
course!

1 Shake the first four ingredients over ice until
well frosted.
2 Strain into a chilled long glass.
3 In a blender, whizz the pineapple with sugar
and 1–2 tbsp of crushed ice to a frothy slush.
4 Float gently on the top of the cocktail.
5 Dress with a slice of strawberry.

mudslide

4–6 cracked ice cubes
1½ measures Kahlúa
1½ measures Bailey's
Irish Cream
1½ measures vodka

SERVES 1

This rather ominous-sounding cocktail is actually a gorgeously creamy and richly-flavoured concoction that is delicious whatever the weather conditions.

1 Put the cracked ice cubes into a cocktail shaker.
2 Pour the Kahlúa, Bailey's Irish Cream and vodka over the ice. Shake vigorously until a frost forms.
3 Strain into a chilled goblet.

snowball classic

1 measure advocaat
good dash fresh lemon juice
ice
lemonade, to top up
slices of orange and lemon,
to decorate

SERVES 1

The familiar golden egg yellow of advocaat is preferred by many when it is lengthened with soda or tonic and given an added tang of lemon.

1 Stir the advocaat and lemon over ice in a mixing glass.
2 Strain into a highball glass filled with ice and top up with lemonade to taste.
3 Dress with slices of orange and lemon.

moonraker

4–6 cracked ice cubes
dash of Pernod
1 measure peach brandy
1 measure brandy
1 measure quinquina

SERVES 1

A powerful mix, this cocktail is more likely to fire you into orbit than to reduce you to trying to rake the moon's reflection out of a pond.

1 Put the cracked ice cubes into a mixing glass. Dash Pernod over the ice and pour in the peach brandy, brandy and quinquina.
2 Stir well to mix, then strain into a chilled highball glass.

banshee

4–6 cracked ice cubes
2 measures crème
de banane
1 measure crème de cacao
1 measure single cream

SERVES 1

A surprising number of cocktails are named after ghouls, ghosts and things that go bump in the night. It seems unlikely that this one will get you wailing (except with delight), but it might make your hair stand on end.

1 Put the cracked ice cubes into a cocktail shaker.
2 Pour the crème de banane, crème de cacao and single cream over the ice. Shake vigorously until a frost forms.
3 Strain into a chilled wine glass.

angel's delight

½ measure grenadine, chilled
½ measure Triple Sec, chilled
½ measure sloe gin, chilled
½ measure single cream, chilled

SERVES 1

This is a modern version of the classic pousse –
café, in that the ingredients form separate
layers in the glass – providing you have a
steady hand – to create a rainbow effect. You
can drink it as a slammer or sip it in a more
genteel manner.

1 Pour the grenadine into a chilled shot glass,
pousse-café glass or champagne flute, then,
with a steady hand, pour in the Triple Sec to
make a second layer.
2 Add the sloe gin to make a third layer and,
finally, add the cream to float on top.

yankee doodle

1 measure crème de banane
1 measure cognac
1 measure Royal
Mint Chocolate
ice

SERVES 1

Serve this delicious concoction after dinner on a
warm summer evening.

1 Shake all three ingredients together over ice
until well frosted and strain into a small cocktail
glass.

stars and swirls

1 measure Malibu
½ measure strawberry or
raspberry liqueur
1 tsp blue Curaçao
ice

SERVES 1

You will need a steady hand for this one –
preferably two pairs of steady hands.

1 Chill a small shot glass really well.
2 Pour in the Malibu and add a large ice cube.
3 Carefully pour in the other two liqueurs from
opposite sides of the glass very slowly so they fall
down the sides and swirl around.

coconut breeze

This cocktail uses clear or white coconut liqueur, but if you can't find it, a creamy coconut liqueur will make a good replacement.

1 measure coconut liqueur
½ measure Drambuie
2 measures papaya juice
few ice cubes
slice of lime, to decorate

SERVES 1

1 Shake the ingredients well over ice until well frosted.
2 Pour into a chilled cocktail glass and finish with a slice of lime.

the chocolate diva

4 cubes good quality milk
chocolate, melted
1 measure Grand Marnier
1 measure vodka
1 measure crème de cacao
1 tbsp fresh orange juice
fresh edible flower (pansy, rose
petals, nasturtium), to decorate

SERVES 1

Chocaholics will not be able to resist this
wicked alcohol and chocolate combination, but
it really needs to be very cold.

1 Mix the melted chocolate gently with the
liqueurs and orange juice until well blended.
2 Pour into a chilled cocktail glass and float a
flower or petals on the top to finish.

candy floss

1 measure peach schnapps
1 measure banana liqueur
1 measure apricot brandy
1–2 measures orange juice
ice
banana, to decorate

SERVES 1

Banana freezes well, so it is great to use as a stirrer or finish to banana cocktails. Cut the fruit into long thin strips or diagonal slices and freeze briefly.

1 Mix the first three ingredients well with orange juice to taste.
2 Pour into a tumbler full of ice and finish with a few pieces of banana, fresh or frozen.

japanese jewel

4–5 green grapes
1–2 tsp egg white,
slightly beaten
caster sugar
1 measure melon liqueur
1 measure gin
2 measures kiwi juice
crushed ice

SERVES 1

Sugared fruits always look spectacular as a finishing touch. Prepared them in advance if you are making several drinks.

1 Pick out the best two grapes to dip in egg white and then sugar. Set aside to dry.
2 Whizz all the rest of the ingredients in a blender with a little crushed ice for about 10 seconds until slushy.
3 Pour into a medium-size cocktail glass with more ice and dress with the two sugared grapes on a cocktail stick.

luisita

1 measure blue Curaçao
lemon barley water
few dashes lemon juice
ice
tonic water
lemon or lime slices,
to decorate

SERVES 1

If you are not feeling in a blue mood remember you can buy orange Curaçao and change the whole mood without changing the taste!

1 Stir the Curaçao, barley water and lemon over ice in a chilled long tumbler.
2 Add tonic water to taste and dress with a few slices of lemon.

napoleon

1 measure Mandarine Napoleon
1 measure cherry brandy
ice
lemonade, to top up

SERVES 1

These two rich fruity liqueurs mix well and make a great long cocktail.

1 Pour the liqueurs into a highball glass filled with ice.
2 Stir gently and then gradually top up with lemonade.

princess

2 tsp chilled single cream
1 tsp caster sugar
2 measures
apricot brandy, chilled

SERVES 1

No particular princess is specified, although a number of other cocktails are named after queens and princes, as well as princesses. Perhaps drinking this makes everyone feel like royalty.

1 Pour the cream into a small bowl and stir in the sugar.
2 Pour the apricot brandy into a chilled liqueur glass and float the sweetened cream on top by pouring it over the back of a teaspoon.

star bangled spanner

½ measure green
Chartreuse, chilled
½ measure Triple Sec, chilled
½ measure cherry
brandy, chilled
½ measure crème
violette, chilled
½ measure yellow
Chartreuse, chilled
½ measure blue Curaçao, chilled
½ measure brandy, chilled

SERVES 1

Although only half measures of each spirit are used, there are seven layers of them, so this is quite a potent cocktail. It is probably fortunate that after getting your tongue around a couple, your hand will become too unsteady to pour more.

1 Pour the green Chartreuse into a chilled champagne flute, then, with a steady hand, gently pour in the Triple Sec to make a second layer.
2 Gently add the cherry brandy to make a third layer, the crème violette to make a fourth, the yellow Chartreuse to make a fifth and the Curaçao to make a sixth.
3 Finally, float the brandy on top.

mocktinis

jersey lily

1 glass sparkling apple juice
sugar to taste
1 dash Angostura bitters
ice cubes
maraschino cherry
and apple slice, to decorate

SERVES 1

This clear, golden refresher is named for the Edwardian beauty, actress Lillie Langtry (1852–1929). Whether the most famous of her lovers, the Prince of Wales (later King Edward VII), enjoyed it too, history does not record.

1 Mix a little sugar into the apple juice, add the bitters and ice cubes and stir until well frosted.
2 Strain into a chilled glass. Spear a thin slice of apple and a cherry on a cocktail stick to garnish or simply drop the cherry into the bottom of the glass.

applesour

4 measures pure apple juice
juice of 1 lemon and 1 lime
1 measure sugar syrup
or clear honey
1 small egg white
crushed ice
4–5 raspberries
long strip apple peel,
to decorate

SERVES 1

The lemon and lime juice give this cocktail more than a hint of sharpness, but it is soon masked by the sweet honey and apple flavours.

1 Whizz all ingredients, except the fruit and peel, in a blender until very frothy and partly frozen.
2 Put three raspberries in the base of an iced tall glass, crush with a wooden spoon and then pour in the fruit slush.
3 Dress with the raspberries and a strip of peel.

little prince

4–6 cracked ice cubes
1 measure apricot juice
1 measure lemon juice
2 measures sparkling
apple juice
twist of lemon peel,
to decorate

SERVES 1

Sparkling apple juice is a particularly useful ingredient in non-alcoholic cocktails because it adds flavour and colour, as well as fizz. Try using it as a substitute for champagne in non-alcoholic versions of such cocktails as Buck's Fizz.

1 Put the cracked ice cubes into a mixing glass.
2 Pour the apricot juice, lemon juice and apple juice over the ice and stir well.
3 Strain into a chilled highball glass and decorate with the lemon twist.

baby love

300ml/10 fl oz cold milk
12–14 strawberries,
washed and hulled
½ ripe avocado
1 measure lemon juice

SERVES 2

Avocado is so luxuriously smooth when
blended that this cocktail risks needing a
spoon, especially if you like it too much.

1 Place all the ingredients (save two
strawberries) in a blender and whizz for 15–20
seconds until smooth.
2 Pour into iced tall glasses and top with a
whole strawberry.

banana coffee break

300ml/10 fl oz milk
4 tbsp instant coffee powder
150g/5oz vanilla ice cream
2 bananas, sliced and frozen
brown sugar, to taste

SERVES 2

Thanks to the coffee, this a very adult-tasting smoothie-style cocktail. In warm weather, it makes an excellent mid-morning pick-me-up.

1 Pour the milk into a food processor, add the coffee powder and process gently until combined.
2 Add half of the vanilla ice cream and process gently, then add the remaining ice cream and process until well combined.
3 When the mixture is thoroughly blended, add the bananas, and sugar to taste, and process until smooth.
4 Pour the mixture into glasses and serve dressed with a few slices of banana.

carrot chill

500ml/17 fl oz carrot juice
30g/1oz watercress
1 tbsp lemon juice
sprigs of fresh watercress,
to decorate

SERVES 2

Carrots have a really sweet flavour, especially very young raw carrots. The juice makes a great combination with the peppery watercress.

1 Pour the carrot juice into a blender.
2 Add the watercress and lemon juice and process until smooth.
3 Transfer to a jug, cover with film and chill in the refrigerator for at least an hour,
4 When thoroughly chilled, pour into glasses and dress with sprigs of fresh watercress. Serve at once.

cherry kiss

8 ice cubes, crushed
2 tbsp cherry syrup
500ml/17 fl oz
sparkling water
2–3 splashes fresh
lime juice
maraschino cherries on
cocktail sticks,
to decorate

SERVES 2

A refreshing and almost calorie-free cocktail, perfect for dieting or simply for one of those non-alcohol occasions.

1 Divide the crushed ice between two glasses and pour the syrup over.
2 Add the lime juice and top up with sparkling water.
3 Decorate with the maraschino cherries on cocktail sticks and serve.

cinnamon tea

400ml/14 fl oz water
4 cloves
1 small stick of cinnamon
2 tea bags
3–4 tbsp lemon juice
1–2 tbsp brown sugar
slices of fresh lemon, to decorate

SERVES 2

If you like herbal or fruit teas you will enjoy this spicy, citrusy tea. It's also good cold.

1 Bring water, cloves and cinnamon to boil.
2 Remove from heat and add tea bags. Leave to infuse 5 minutes, then remove.
3 Stir in lemon juice, sugar and extra hot water to taste.
4 Heat through again gently and strain into heatproof glasses.
5 Decorate with slices of fresh lemon and serve. Serve chilled if you prefer.

cocobelle

3 measures cold milk
1 measure coconut cream
2 scoops vanilla ice cream
3–4 ice cubes
dash grenadine
long-shred coconut, toasted,
to decorate

SERVES 1

If you have a steady hand, this drink can be served with pretty swirls of colour up the sides. Youngsters will no doubt be keen to help you with this one!

1 Whizz the first four ingredients in a blender until slushy.
2 Chill a tall glass and gently dribble a few splashes of grenadine down the insides.
3 Pour in the slush slowly so not all the colour is dissolved immediately and sprinkle with toasted coconut or flakes of fresh coconut.

mocha slush

4–6 crushed ice cubes
2 measures coffee syrup
1 measure chocolate syrup
4 measures milk
grated chocolate, to decorate

SERVES 1

Definitely for people with a sweet tooth, this is a chocoholic's dream and is popular with adults, as well as children.

1 Put the crushed ice cubes into a blender and add the coffee syrup, chocolate syrup and milk. Blend until slushy.
2 Pour into a chilled goblet and sprinkle with grated chocolate.

cranberry punch

A sophisticated, non-alcoholic punch. Serve hot for a winter party or chilled for a summer celebration.

600ml/1 pint cranberry juice
600ml/1 pint orange juice
150ml/5 fl oz water
½ tsp ground ginger
¼ tsp ground cinnamon
¼ tsp freshly grated nutmeg
cracked ice cubes or
block of ice, optional

To decorate (cold punch):
fresh cranberries
1 egg white, lightly beaten
caster sugar
sprigs of fresh mint

To decorate (hot punch):
slices of lemon
slices of orange

SERVES 10

1 For a cold punch, first prepare the decoration. Dip the cranberries in the egg white, then roll them in the sugar to frost. Set aside on baking paper to dry. Repeat with the mint leaves.
2 Put the cranberry juice, orange juice, water, ginger, cinnamon and nutmeg in a saucepan and bring to the boil. Lower the heat and simmer for 5 minutes.
3 If serving hot, pour into a warmed punch bowl. Decorate with lemon and orange.
4 To serve cold, set aside to cool, then refrigerate for at least two hours. Decorate with the frosted cranberries and mint leaves.

grapefruit cooler

50g/2oz fresh mint
2 measures sugar syrup
475ml/16 fl oz grapefruit juice
4 measures lemon juice
cracked ice cubes
sparkling mineral water
sprigs of fresh mint, to decorate

SERVES 6

Start making this at least two hours before you want to serve it to allow plenty of time for the mint to infuse in the syrup.

1 Muddle fresh mint leaves in a small bowl with the sugar syrup.

2 Set aside for at least two hours to infuse, mashing again from time to time.

3 Strain into a jug and add the grapefruit juice and lemon juice.

4 Cover with film and chill for at least two hours until required.

5 To serve, fill six chilled Collins glasses with cracked ice.

6 Divide the cocktail between the glasses and top up with sparkling water.

7 Dress with fresh mint.

soft sangria

1½ litres/2¾ pints
red grape juice
300ml/10 fl oz orange juice
3 measures cranberry juice
2 measures lemon juice
2 measures lime juice
4 measures sugar syrup
block of ice
slices of lemon, orange and
lime, to decorate

SERVES 20

This is a version of the well-known Spanish wine
cup that has caught out many an unwary
tourist because it seems so innocuous, whereas
it is actually very potent. A Soft Sangria poses
no such danger of unexpected inebriation, but
is just as refreshing and flavoursome. Make sure
all the ingredients are thoroughly chilled before
mixing them.

1 Put the grape juice, orange juice, cranberry
juice, lemon juice, lime juice and sugar syrup
into a chilled punch bowl and stir well.
2 Add the ice and decorate with the slices of
lemon, orange and lime.

italian soda

6–8 cracked ice cubes
1–1½ measures hazelnut syrup
sparkling mineral water,
to top up
slice of lime, to decorate

SERVES 1

Available from Italian delicatessens and some
supermarkets, Italian syrup comes in a wide
variety of flavours, including a range of fruit
and nuts. French syrups are similar and also
include many different flavours. You can
substitute your favourite for the hazelnut used
here and vary the quantity depending on how
sweet you like your drinks.

1 Fill a chilled Collins glass with cracked ice
cubes.
2 Pour the hazelnut syrup over the ice and top
up with sparkling mineral water.
3 Stir gently and decorate with the lime slice.

lassi

150ml/5 fl oz plain yoghurt
450ml/15 fl oz milk
1 tbsp rose water
3 tbsp honey
1 ripe mango, peeled and diced
6 ice cubes
rose petals (optional),
to decorate

SERVES 2

Originally Lassi was simply a flavoured yoghurt drink, slightly soured, often savoury or spiced. There are many delicious drinks you can make from it.

1 Pour the yoghurt and milk into a processor and process gently until combined.
2 Add the rose water and honey and process until thoroughly blended, then add the mango and ice cubes and continue blending until smooth.
3 Pour into chilled glasses and dress with edible petals (if using).

slush puppy

juice 1 lemon or ½ pink
grapefruit
½ measure grenadine
ice
few strips lemon peel
2–3 tsp raspberry syrup
soda water, to taste
maraschino cherry,
to decorate

SERVES 1

Pink, pretty and refreshing – it looks serious, but you won't need to book a taxi home.

1 Pour the lemon juice and grenadine into a chilled tall glass with ice.
2 Add lemon peel, syrup and soda water to taste. Finish off with a cherry.

sober sunday

1 measure grenadine
1 measure fresh lemon
or lime juice
ice
lemonade, to top up
slices of lemon and lime,
to decorate

SERVES 1

An interesting variation for those not drinking and any who are driving.

1 Pour the grenadine and fruit juice into an ice-filled highball glass.
2 Top up with lemonade and finish with slices of lemon and lime.

shirley temple

8–10 cracked ice cubes
2 measures lemon juice
½ measure grenadine
½ measure sugar syrup
ginger ale, to top up
slice of orange,
cocktail cherry,
to decorate

SERVES 1

This is one of the most famous of classic non-alcoholic cocktails. Shirley Temple Black became a respected diplomat, but this cocktail dates from the days when she was an immensely popular child film star in the 1930s.

1 Put 4–6 cracked ice cubes into a cocktail shaker.
2 Pour the lemon juice, grenadine and sugar syrup over the ice and shake vigorously.
3 Half fill a small, chilled glass with cracked ice cubes and strain the cocktail over them. Top up with ginger ale. Decorate with an orange slice and a cocktail cherry.

muddy puddle

juice ½ lemon
juice ½ orange
crushed ice
cola, chilled, to top up
slice of orange,
to decorate

SERVES 1

Reminiscent of the mess one's children make when mixing drinks! Well, in fact that's just how this murky-looking but surprisingly refreshing drink was created.

1 Pour the fruit juice over crushed ice in a chilled long glass and top up with the well-iced cola.
2 Finish with a slice of orange and a serve with a straw.

raspberry lemonade

2 lemons
100g/4oz caster sugar
100g/4oz fresh raspberries
few drops vanilla essence
crushed ice
sparkling water, iced,
to top up
sprigs of lemon balm, to
decorate

SERVES 4

If you like real old-fashioned lemonade, then you will love this version.

1 Trim the ends off the lemons, scoop out and chop the flesh and place in a blender with the sugar, raspberries, vanilla and ice.
2 Blend for 2–3 minutes or until there are no lumps.
3 Strain into tall glasses and top up with ice cubes and water. Finish with sprigs of lemon balm.

tropical delight

2 large ripe mangoes
1 tbsp icing sugar
600ml/1 pint coconut milk
5 ice cubes
flaked toasted coconut,
to decorate

SERVES 4

A velvety-smooth, delicately scented drink without alcohol. This can be served at any time of day – and it's delicious for breakfast.

1 Peel the mangoes, coarsely chop the flesh and discard the stones.
2 Place the flesh in a blender with the sugar and blend until completely smooth.
3 Add the coconut milk and ice to the blender and process until frothy.
4 Pour into four tall glasses and sprinkle with flaked toasted coconut to serve.

melon medley

4–6 crushed ice cubes
60g/2oz diced melon flesh
4 measures orange juice
½ measure lemon juice

SERVES 1

Choose a very ripe, sweet-fleshed melon, such as a cantaloupe, for this lovely, fresh-tasting cocktail. This drink is perfect for sipping on a hot evening.

1 Put the crushed ice cubes into a blender and add the diced melon. Pour in the orange juice and lemon juice. Blend until slushy.
2 Pour into a chilled Collins glass.

mint and cucumber refresher

few sprigs mint
1 tsp caster sugar
juice 1 lime
1in/2cm piece cucumber, thinly sliced
your favourite sparkling water, chilled, to taste

SERVES 1

Put this top of the list when you next go on a diet – it's the perfect booster.

1 Chop a few mint leaves and mix with sugar.
2 Rub a little lime juice round the rim of a pretty glass and dip in the minted sugar. Leave to dry.
3 Mix the rest of the lime juice, cucumber and mint – some chopped and some whole – in a jug and chill.
4 To serve, pour lime and cucumber into the prepared glass and top up with chilled water to taste.

juicy julep

1 measure orange juice
1 measure pineapple juice
1 measure lime juice
½ measure raspberry syrup
4 crushed fresh mint leaves
cracked ice cubes
ginger ale, to top up
fresh sprig of mint, to decorate

SERVES 1

Taken from the Arabic word, which in turn was derived from Persian, meaning rose water, it seems likely that julep was always a non-alcoholic drink until imaginative bourbon-drinking Derby-goers hijacked the term.

1 Shake the orange juice, pineapple juice, lime juice and raspberry syrup with the mint leaves vigorously over ice until well frosted.
2 Strain into a chilled Collins glass, top up with ginger ale and stir gently.
3 Dress with a sprig of fresh mint.

island cooler

8–10 cracked ice cubes
2 measures orange juice
1 measure lemon juice
1 measure pineapple juice
1 measure papaya juice
½ tsp grenadine
sparkling mineral water,
to top up
pineapple wedges,
cocktail cherries, to decorate

SERVES 1

Nothing could be more refreshing on a hot summer's day than this colourful combination of tropical fruit juices. To get into a party mood, go to town and decorate with a cocktail parasol, swizzle stick and straws, as well as fresh fruit.

1 Put 4–6 cracked ice cubes into a cocktail shaker. Pour the orange juice, lemon juice, pineapple juice, papaya juice and grenadine over the ice. Shake vigorously until a frost forms.
2 Half fill a chilled Collins glass with cracked ice cubes and pour the cocktail over them. Top up with sparkling mineral water and stir gently. Decorate with pineapple wedges and cocktail cherries speared on a cocktail stick.

citrus fizz

2 measures fresh
orange juice, chilled
caster sugar
few drops Angostura bitters
squeeze lime juice
2–3 measures sparkling
water, chilled, to taste

SERVES 1

This is a clever and refreshing variation on the classic Buck's Fizz, which is perfect for all ages in the family.

1 Rub the rim of a flute with orange or lime juice and dip into caster sugar.
2 Stir the rest of the juices together with the bitters and then pour into the glass.
3 Top up with sparkling water to taste.

cinders

juice ½ orange
juice 1 lime
150ml/5 fl oz pineapple juice
several drops Angostura bitters
ice
soda water or dry
ginger, to taste
slices of orange and
pineapple, to decorate

SERVES 1

Yes, it's non-alcoholic but no-one needs to
know if you dress it up well.

1 Shake the first four ingredients well together
with ice.
2 Strain into a chilled glass and top up with
soda water to taste.
3 Finish with a few more drops Angostura
bitters and sliced fruit.

sweet dreamer

1 measure orange juice
2 measures passion fruit
nectar or juice
1 small banana
¼ ripe mango or papaya
few drops vanilla essence
crushed ice

SERVES 2

Wonderfully creamy and thick with fruit and
goodness, the perfect wake up package or
early evening settler.

1 Whizz all the ingredients together in a
blender or processor until smooth and yet
slushy.
2 Pour into large cocktail glasses or goblets.

california smoothie

1 banana, peeled and
thinly sliced
60g/2oz strawberries
90g/3oz stoned dates
4½ tsp clear honey
250ml/9 fl oz orange juice
4–6 crushed ice cubes

SERVES 1

Smoothies of all sorts – alcoholic and non-alcoholic – have become immensely popular in the last two or three years. The secret of success is to blend them on medium speed until just smooth.

1 Put the banana, strawberries, dates and honey into a blender and blend until smooth.
2 Add the orange juice and crushed ice cubes and blend again until smooth. Pour into a chilled Collins glass.

eye of the hurricane

4–6 cracked ice cubes
2 measures passion fruit syrup
1 measure lime juice
bitter lemon, to top up
slice of lemon, to decorate

SERVES 1

In recent years, a vast range of fruit juices and syrups has become widely available. These can extend the range of the cocktail bar and are particularly useful for non-alcoholic mixed drinks, which were once heavily dependent on the rather tired old favourites of orange, lemon and lime juices.

1 Put the cracked ice cubes into a mixing glass.
2 Pour the syrup and lime juice over the ice and stir well to mix.
3 Strain into a chilled tumbler and top up with bitter lemon. Stir gently and decorate with the lemon slice.

pineapple smoothie

125m/4 fl oz pineapple juice
juice of 1 lemon
100ml/3½ fl oz water
3 tbsp brown sugar
175ml/6 fl oz natural yoghurt
1 peach, cut into
chunks and frozen
100g/4oz frozen
pineapple chunks
wedges of fresh pineapple,
to decorate

SERVES 2

This is a popular combination for a smoothie –
one smooth sweet fruit and one tangy and
textured fruit. You might like to try your own
variation.

1 Blend all the ingredients, except the pineapple
wedges, in a food processor until smooth.
2 Pour into glasses and dress the rims with
wedges of fresh pineapple.

angelina

2 measures orange juice
10 pineapple cubes
a few ice cubes
splash of raspberry or
strawberry cordial or syrup

SERVES 1

Use canned pineapple in this recipe and you are
bound to be tempted to make some of this
delicious concoction for all the family, too.

1 Whizz the first three ingredients in a blender
for about 10 seconds until frothy and well mixed.
2 Put a good splash of cordial in the base of a
chilled long glass and slowly pour in the cocktail.
3 Splash with a little more cordial and drink with
a straw.

faux kir

1 measure raspberry
syrup, chilled
white grape juice, chilled,
to top up

SERVES 1

A non-alcoholic version of the classic wine
cocktail, this drink is just as colourful and tasty.
French and Italian fruit syrups are often the
best quality and have the most flavour.

1 Pour the raspberry syrup into a chilled
wine glass.
2 Top up with the grape juice.
3 Stir well to mix.

strawberry delight

1 measure lemon juice
1 measure orange juice
2–3 strawberries, mashed
1 measure fraise
½ egg yolk
dash grenadine
ice
slice of strawberry,
to decorate

SERVES 1

This is just as delicious made with raspberries
and framboise liqueur.

1 Shake all the ingredients really well together.
2 Pour into a cocktail glass and finish with a
slice of strawberry.

clam digger

10–12 cracked ice cubes
Tabasco sauce
Worcestershire sauce
4 measures tomato juice
4 measures clam juice
¼ tsp horseradish sauce
celery salt and freshly ground
black pepper
celery stick, wedge of lime,
to decorate

SERVES 1

This is another good cocktail for a Sunday brunch, when alcoholic drinks can be too soporific and you end up wasting the rest of the day, but you still want something to wake up the taste buds and set them tingling.

1 Put 4–6 cracked ice cubes into a cocktail shaker. Dash the Tabasco sauce and Worcestershire sauce over the ice, pour in the tomato juice and clam juice and add the horseradish sauce. Shake vigorously until a frost forms.
2 Fill a chilled Collins glass with cracked ice cubes and strain the cocktail over them. Season to taste with celery salt and pepper and decorate with a celery stick and lime wedge.

bloody january

4–6 crushed ice cubes
1 medium red pepper, deseeded
and roughly chopped
2 large tomatoes, peeled,
deseeded and roughly chopped
1 fresh green chilli, deseeded
juice of 1 lime
salt and freshly ground black
pepper
celery stick, to decorate

SERVES 1

Generally, the best non-alcoholic cocktails are originals rather than pale and often insipid copies of their traditional, alcoholic cousins. This non-alcoholic version of the Bloody Mary is one of the exceptions and has some of the kick of the classic cocktail.

1 Put the crushed ice cubes into a blender and add the red pepper, tomatoes, chilli and lime juice. Blend until smooth.
2 Pour into a chilled highball glass and season to taste with salt and pepper. Decorate with a celery stick.

cocktail index

Golden Galleon	109
Hayden's Milk Float	101
Mai Tai	48
Nirvana	106
Pinacolada	53
Planter's Punch	51
Rum Cooler	102
Yellow Bird	105
Zombie	47

TEQUILA

Bombshell	124
Brave Bull	62
Carolina	119
Coco Loco	122
El Diablo	121
Huatusco Whammer	119
Margarita	64
Mexican Fizz	178
Teaser	117
Tequila Mockingbird	122
Tequila Slammer	165
Tequila Steeler	120
Tequila Sunrise	63

VODKA

Angelic	82
Anouchka	91
Bay Breeze	80
Black Russian	36
Bloody Mary	38
Chilly Willy	78
Cinnamon Park	85
Cosmopolitan	30
Crocodile	90
Dry Smile	83
Full Monty	85
Fuzzy Navel	32
Golden Tang	78
Harvey Wallbanger	37

Kamikaze	35
Long Island Iced Tea	38
Moscow Mule	35
Polynesian Pepper Pot	88
Russian Double	87
Salty Dog	32
Screwdriver	30
Sea Breeze	81
Seeing Red	88
Vodga	86
Vodkatini	77

WINE/SHERRY/ FORTIFIED WINES

Adonis	125
Americano	116
Raffles	115
Sherry Cobbler	64
Triple Champion	114
Watermelon Man	127

WHISKY

19th Green	95
Algonquin, The	93
Black Watch	98
Blood and Sand	42
Dandy	96
Godfather	94
Highland Fling	101
Irish Shillelagh	96
Manhattan	45
Mint Julep	46
Mount Etna	99
Old Fashioned	41
Rusty Nail	40
Twin Peaks	93
Whiskey Sour	45
Whisky Mac	42